CHATELAINE
food express
Sizzlers

Sizzlers

OVER 200 BARBECUE RECIPES
WITH INDOOR METHODS FOR YEAR-ROUND ENJOYMENT

BY MONDA ROSENBERG

M&S

A SMITH SHERMAN BOOK
produced in conjunction with CHATELAINE®
and published by McCLELLAND & STEWART INC.

CHATELAINE

Canadian Cataloguing in Publication Data

Rosenberg, Monda
    Sizzlers: over 200 barbecue recipes with indoor methods for year-round enjoyment

(Chatelaine food express)
"A Smith Sherman book produced in conjunction with Chatelaine"
Includes index

ISBN 0-7710-2007-4

1. Barbecue cookery. I. Title II. Series
TX840.B3R673 1998   641.7'6   C98-930399-3

ACKNOWLEDGEMENTS

No one writes a book alone and this one was produced by a caring, talented, hard-working team. I am indebted to Carol Sherman and Andrew Smith who put this book together and made it look so beautiful. Joseph Gisini for his meticulous attention to design detail. Bernice Eisenstein for her eagle-eyed copy editing and Debra Sherman who accurately input the recipes.
At CHATELAINE, thanks to Marilyn Crowley and Trudy Patterson, who tested the recipes to perfection; Deborah Aldcorn for her smart editing; Rona Maynard for her never-failing, very generous support and editorial eye; and Lee Simpson for her concern and encouragement. For the outstanding photographs, thanks to creative director Miriam Gee and superb food stylist Rosemarie Superville; photographers Ed O'Neil and Michael Mahovlich; CHATELAINE art director Caren Watkins and creative associate Barbara Glaser. Many thanks to Alison Fryer and Jennifer Grange from The Cookbook Store for their superb marketing advice.And thanks to everyone at McClelland and Stewart, especially Pat Kennedy.

MONDA ROSENBERG

COVER PHOTO: MAPLE CHICKEN AND GRILLED FRUIT, *see recipe page 51*

PHOTO PAGE 2: FISH & CHIPS ON THE BARBIE, *see recipe page 61*

CREDITS: *see page 143*

PRINTED AND BOUND IN CANADA

2 3 4 5   02 01 00 99

WE LOVE TO BARBECUE. IT'S THE MOST RELAXED WAY TO COOK AND ENTERTAIN, AND NOW IT JUST GOT BETTER.

Grill all year long with *Sizzlers*, the second book in the CHATELAINE FOOD EXPRESS series. The same elements that made *Quickies*, our first book, a bestseller are here again. Finding the recipes is a snap with our handy alphabetical sections from Beef to Xtras. Ingredients are highlighted for easy use. And because we know it's not always practical to barbecue, we've also included indoor oven instructions for many of the recipes.

Everybody knows about tossing hamburgers and hot dogs on the grill, but now learn about potato salads, lamb roasts, and vegetables that take centre stage to star in salads and salsas. And yes, the basic burger is here too, with lots of other burger recipes and toppings

Sizzlers provides quick ways to add panache to all your favorites. Look for fast weekday grills or more sophisticated entrées when you want to impress. There's a classy French steak sizzler, chock-full of shallots and Dijon, a lamb burger aromatic with cumin and coriander, an amazing vegetable salad, sure to be the hit of any get-together. Fish is a natural, especially when you want to eat light. Ribs are always a treat for neighborhood gatherings or big family reunions. We've even got an entire section of items you probably never thought to put on the grill, including mussels, corned beef and sublime liver and onions. Flavors from Asia, the Caribbean, the Mediterranean and other exotic locales highlight many of the recipes.

Sizzlers gives you more than 200 tasty reasons to fire up the barbecue — plus more than 70 indoor adaptations for year-round enjoyment.

CONTENTS

BEEF

*A great steak needs little embellishment.
This smashing-looking PRIME PEPPER SIRLOIN
(see recipe page 10) heeds that advice.
A top sirloin (used here) is a great tender steak
to buy, but use whatever steak is on special.*

PRIME PEPPER SIRLOIN

A double combo of seductive green and pungent cracked black peppercorns adds an assertive touch.

Oil grill and preheat barbecue.
Trim fat and nick edges to prevent curling from
   2 lbs (1 kg) sirloin, rib-eye or strip-loin steak,
    at least 1 inch (2.5 cm) thick
Sprinkle onto both sides of meat
   2 tbsp green peppercorns in brine,
    drained and finely chopped
   1 tsp cracked black peppercorns
Place steak on grill. Barbecue, uncovered, for 8
   minutes. Then turn and continue barbecuing
   for 5 to 8 more minutes for medium-rare.
Let stand for 5 minutes before cutting into
   individual portions. Steak is great with
   Tomato & Hot Pepper Salsa or Pesto
   Tomatoes (see recipes pages 111 and 120).
Makes: 4 to 6 servings

PREPARATION: 15 MINUTES
GRILL: 16 MINUTES

INDOOR SIZZLE:
For oven broiling, see below.

SESAME CORIANDER STEAK

A sesame-garlic baste and a squeeze of lime give a touch of Oriental flair to a basic steak.

Oil grill and preheat barbecue. Stir together
   2 tbsp sesame oil, preferably dark
   1 crushed garlic clove
   ½ tsp salt
   ¼ tsp cayenne pepper
Brush over
   2 lbs (1 kg) sirloin, rib-eye or flank steak,
    at least ¾ inch (2 cm) thick
Grill steak until seared, about 4 to 6 minutes per
   side for medium-rare, or until done as you
   like. Place on a cutting board. Immediately
   squeeze
   juice of 2 limes
   over hot steak and sprinkle with
   ¼ cup chopped fresh coriander
Thinly slice meat across grain. Serve with Black
   Bean 'n' Pepper Salsa (see recipe page 111).
   It's also wonderful stirred in a salad or
   wrapped in warm tortillas.
Makes: 6 servings

PREPARATION: 5 MINUTES
GRILL: 12 MINUTES

INDOOR BROILING FOR YEAR-ROUND SIZZLE

Where a recipe indicates Indoor Sizzle, prepare steak as directed, but when it's time to barbecue, use this oven method instead. Preheat oven broiler. Place steak on a broiler pan about 4 inches (10 cm) from broiler. Broil, about 4 to 6 minutes per side for medium-rare for ¾-inch (2-cm) thick steak; 5 to 8 minutes per side for 1-inch (2.5-cm) thick steak; and 7 to 12 minutes for 1½-inch (4-cm) thick steak.

EASY EASTERN STEAK

*A lemon-soy marinade that doesn't need any fancy ingredients
turns economical flank steak into a special entrée.*

Whisk together
  2 to 3 tbsp soy sauce
  2 tbsp lemon juice
  2 tbsp olive oil
  1 tbsp brown sugar
  1 crushed garlic clove
  generous grinding of black pepper

Place
  1 lb (500 g) flank or top round steak,
    at least ¾ inch (2 cm) thick
in a shallow dish just large enough to snugly
hold it or in a large self-sealing bag. Pour
lemon-soy mixture over top. Cover dish or
seal bag. Leave at room temperature for
1 hour or refrigerate overnight.

Oil grill and preheat barbecue. Grill steak for 4 to
6 minutes per side for medium-rare. Then
slice diagonally and serve with fresh cole slaw
and mushrooms.
Makes: 4 servings

PREPARATION: 10 MINUTES
MARINATE: 1 HOUR
GRILL: 12 MINUTES

INDOOR SIZZLE:
For oven broiling, see page 10.

EASY EASTERN STEAK

BEEF

SIZZLING SOUTH-OF-THE-BORDER STEAK

For a sensational Tex-Mex flavor hit, let your steak languish in this spicy lime marinade.

In a small bowl, whisk together
   1/4 cup freshly squeezed lime juice
   1/3 cup vegetable or olive oil
   3 crushed garlic cloves
   1 tsp chili powder
   1 tsp cumin
   1/2 tsp dried leaf oregano
   1/2 tsp freshly ground black pepper
   1/2 tsp hot pepper sauce
   1/4 tsp salt

Place
   2 lbs (1 kg) flank or porterhouse steak,
      at least 3/4 inch (2 cm) thick
   in a shallow dish just large enough to snugly
   hold it or in a large self-sealing bag. Pour lime
   mixture over top. Cover dish or seal bag.
   Leave at room temperature for 1 hour or
   refrigerate for 4 hours.

Oil grill and preheat barbecue. Barbecue steak
   for 4 to 6 minutes per side for medium-rare.

Let stand for 5 minutes before slicing diagonally.
   Serve steak slices with a tossed salad or
   wrapped in tortillas warmed on the barbecue.
   Makes: 8 servings

PREPARATION: 10 MINUTES
MARINATE: 1 HOUR
GRILL: 12 MINUTES

INDOOR SIZZLE:
For oven broiling, see page 10.

MEDITERRANEAN STEAK

A juicy, garlicky steak, hot off the grill, is the perfect companion for a big Greek salad.

Whisk together
   1/4 cup olive oil
   2 tbsp freshly squeezed lemon juice
   2 crushed garlic cloves
   1/2 tsp hot red pepper flakes
   1/4 tsp freshly ground black pepper
   dash of hot pepper sauce

Place
   1 1/2 lbs (750 g) top round, sirloin or
      rib-eye steak, at least 1 inch (2.5 cm) thick
   in a shallow dish just large enough to snugly
   hold it or in a large self-sealing bag. Pour
   lemon mixture over top. Cover dish or
   seal bag. Leave at room temperature for
   30 minutes. Turn several times.

Oil grill and preheat barbecue. Place steak on
   grill. Barbecue, uncovered, for 5 to 8 minutes
   per side for medium-rare.

Let stand for 5 minutes before slicing diagonally.
   Serve with thinly sliced barbecued potatoes
   and sautéed or grilled peppers.
   Makes: 6 servings

PREPARATION: 5 MINUTES
MARINATE: 30 MINUTES
GRILL: 16 MINUTES

INDOOR SIZZLE:
For oven broiling, see page 10.

Asian Ginger Chili Steak

Create an intriguing spicy Oriental steak with this easy marinade that takes 5 minutes to make.

Whisk together

    3 tbsp soy sauce
    2 tbsp red wine vinegar
    2 tbsp vegetable oil
    1 tbsp brown sugar
    1 tbsp grated fresh ginger
    ½ tsp hot red pepper flakes

Place

    1½ lbs (750 g) flank steak,
        at least ¾ inch (2 cm) thick

in a shallow dish just large enough to snugly hold it or in a large self-sealing bag. Pour soy mixture over top. Cover dish or seal bag. Leave at room temperature for 1 hour or refrigerate overnight. Turn several times during marinating.

Oil grill and preheat barbecue. Barbecue steak about 4 to 6 minutes per side for medium-rare.

Thinly slice steak crosswise and serve immediately with Sweet 'n' Sour Cucumber Salsa (see recipe page 110).

Makes: 6 servings

PREPARATION: 5 MINUTES
MARINATE: 1 HOUR
GRILL: 12 MINUTES

INDOOR SIZZLE:
For oven broiling, see page 10.

Caesar Steaks

Two great tastes are paired together here — grilled steak infused with a bold Caesar dressing.

Oil grill and preheat barbecue. Whisk together

    3 tbsp vegetable oil
    1 tbsp anchovy paste
    4 large crushed garlic cloves
    2 tsp Worcestershire sauce
    1 tsp coarsely ground black pepper

Brush over

    4 tender steaks, such as filet mignon or
        rib eye, at least 1 inch (2.5 cm) thick

Place steaks on grill and barbecue for 5 to 8 minutes per side for medium-rare. Serve with Roasted Red Pepper Sauce (see recipe page 110).

Makes: 4 servings

PREPARATION: 5 MINUTES
GRILL: 16 MINUTES

INDOOR SIZZLE:
For oven broiling, see page 10.

Caesar Steaks

BEEF

THAI STEAK & POTATOES

The zing in chili-garlic sauce takes steak and potatoes way beyond its stodgy image.

Make a slit in
    4 unpeeled baking potatoes
and place on a paper towel in microwave. Microwave, uncovered, on high, until partly softened, from 12 to 14 minutes. Or bake 30 minutes in a 400°F (200°C) oven. Cut in half lengthwise and lightly score cut surface.
Oil grill and preheat barbecue. Brush potatoes all over with
    1 tbsp dark sesame oil
and season with
    salt and pepper
Grill, turning occasionally, until lightly golden, from 10 to 15 minutes.
Meanwhile, stir together
    2 tbsp soy sauce
    1 tbsp sesame oil
    1 tbsp chili-garlic sauce
      or Sambal Oelek (a fiery chili sauce)
Brush on both sides of
    2 large rib-eye or strip-loin steaks,
      at least 1 inch (2.5 cm) thick,
      each about ¾ lb (375 g)
Grill steaks for 5 to 8 minutes per side for medium-rare, brushing often with sauce.
Makes: 4 servings

PREPARATION: 15 MINUTES
MICROWAVE: 14 MINUTES
GRILL: 16 MINUTES

SUPERB GRILLED GARLIC STEAK

You don't get much better than this for a classic steak recipe.

Oil grill and preheat barbecue. Stir together
    2 tbsp Dijon mustard
    1 tsp Worcestershire sauce
    2 crushed garlic cloves
    ½ tsp cracked black pepper
Barbecue
    6 rib-eye, sirloin or eye-of-round steaks,
      at least ¾ inch (2 cm) thick
    for 3 minutes per side.
Then brush Dijon-Worcestershire sauce over both sides of steak and continue barbecuing for 2 more minutes per side.
Makes: 6 servings

PREPARATION: 10 MINUTES
GRILL: 10 MINUTES

GARLIC-PEPPER STEAK

Grill one large thick steak and thinly slice across the grain for six hearty servings.

Oil grill and preheat barbecue.
Nick edges of
    2 lbs (1 kg) top round steak,
      at least 1½ inches (4 cm) thick
Rub all over
    1 tbsp vegetable or olive oil
Press into both sides a mixture of
    2 crushed garlic cloves
    1 tbsp coarsely ground pepper
Barbecue for 16 to 20 minutes for rare, turning partway through.
Let stand 5 minutes before slicing diagonally.
Makes: 6 servings

PREPARATION: 10 MINUTES
GRILL: 20 MINUTES

INDOOR SIZZLE:
For oven broiling, see page 10.

GRILLED TEXAS BEEF

An easy mix of four seasonings delivers an incredible robust Tex-Mex taste to any steak.

Oil grill and preheat barbecue. Slice
  6 eye-of-round steaks,
    about 1 inch (2.5 cm) thick
Stir together
  1 tsp ground cumin
  ½ tsp chili powder
  ¼ tsp each cayenne pepper and garlic powder
Evenly sprinkle over steaks, then press into meat.
Place on barbecue and grill for 5 to 8 minutes per
  side for medium-rare.
  Makes: 6 servings

PREPARATION: *5 MINUTES*
GRILL: *16 MINUTES*

INDOOR SIZZLE:
For oven broiling, see page 10.

ROBUST DIJON STEAK

Strip-loin and rib-eye steaks, the ultimate choice for grilling, get a flavor boost from zesty mustard sauce.

Oil grill and preheat barbecue. Stir together
  2 tbsp Dijon mustard
  2 tsp coarsely ground black pepper
  1 tsp Worcestershire sauce
Spread mixture over both sides of
  4 strip-loin or rib-eye steaks
  and place on grill. Barbecue for 5 to 8 minutes
  per side for medium-rare.
  Makes: 4 servings

PREPARATION: *5 MINUTES*
GRILL: *16 MINUTES*

INDOOR SIZZLE:
For oven broiling, see page 10.

BEEF

ROBUST DIJON STEAK

TERRIFIC THAI STEAK

Here's a healthy barbecue entrée that capitalizes on ginger and other assertive flavors from Thailand.

In a small bowl, whisk together
  ¼ cup chili-garlic sauce
    or Sambal Oelek (a fiery chili sauce)
  ¼ cup fish sauce
  1 tbsp sesame oil
  1 tbsp grated fresh ginger
  2 crushed garlic cloves
Place
  2 lbs (1 kg) flank, top round or sirloin steak,
    not more than 1 inch (2.5 cm) thick
  in a shallow dish just large enough to snugly
  hold it or in a large self-sealing bag. Pour
  garlic mixture over top. Cover dish or seal
  bag. Leave at room temperature for 1 hour or
  refrigerate for several hours.
Oil grill and preheat barbecue. Grill steak over
  the hottest part of the barbecue until seared
  and browned, about 5 to 8 minutes per side
  for medium-rare. (Flank steak cooked
  beyond medium tends to be tough.)
Remove steak from barbecue to a cutting board.
  Squeeze over top
  juice of 1 lime
Let stand 5 minutes, then scatter with
  ¼ cup chopped fresh coriander
Thinly slice meat across the grain. Serve with rice
  pilaf or wrapped in warm tortillas topped
  with a dab of sour cream.
Makes: 4 to 6 servings

PREPARATION: 10 MINUTES
MARINATE: 1 HOUR
GRILL: 16 MINUTES

INDOOR SIZZLE:
For oven broiling, see page 10.

SANTA FE BEEF SALAD

Use whatever tender steak you like for this party salad with fiery lime-chili dressing.

Place on a lightly greased barbecue
  3 lbs (1.5 kg) steak, about
    1 inch (2.5 cm) thick
Grill about 5 to 8 minutes per side for
  medium-rare.
Meanwhile, in a large bowl, stir together
  ½ cup freshly squeezed lime juice
  ½ cup granulated sugar
  ¼ cup olive or vegetable oil
  4 large crushed garlic cloves
  1 tsp hot red pepper flakes
  4 green onions, thinly sliced
  ½ tsp salt
  ¼ tsp freshly ground black pepper
Cover a platter or 10 individual plates with
  16 cups mixed salad greens
When meat is grilled, thinly slice diagonally
  across the grain. Cut into bite-size pieces.
  Immediately toss with dressing. Stir in
  2 red peppers, seeded and julienned
Serve warm on greens with chopped coriander,
  avocado slices and grilled tortilla wedges.
Makes: 10 servings

PREPARATION: 20 MINUTES
GRILL: 16 MINUTES

INDOOR SIZZLE:
For oven broiling, see page 10.

Garlic Steak

When you feel the urge to add something special to your steak before it hits the grill, try this instant dress-up. Serve with Pesto Tomatoes (see recipe page 120).

Oil grill and preheat barbecue. Coarsely grind and press
   black pepper
   over both sides of
   2 steaks, such as rib eye, strip loin or sirloin,
      about 1 inch (2.5 cm) thick
Place steaks on grill and top each steak with a small dab of
   cold garlic butter,
      homemade or store-bought
As soon as it starts to melt, spread evenly over the top of meat so it won't run off sides.

When first side of steaks are done as you like, after 5 to 8 minutes, turn over and spread top surface with garlic butter. Continue grilling until done, from 5 to 8 more minutes. Remove to heated plates. Place a cold square of garlic butter on top of each hot steak just before serving.

Makes: 2 servings

PREPARATION: 5 MINUTES
GRILL: 16 MINUTES

GARLIC STEAK WITH PESTO TOMATOES

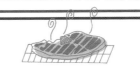

BEEF

GRILLED FAJITA STEAK

For a fun meal, wrap barbecued steak strips and saucy toppings in warm tortillas.

Preheat barbecue. Place
  2 lbs (1 kg) sirloin, strip-loin or flank steak in a shallow dish just large enough to snugly hold it or in a large self-sealing bag.
In a small bowl, whisk together
  ½ cup freshly squeezed lime juice
  ¼ cup red wine vinegar
  ¼ cup vegetable or olive oil
  6 crushed garlic cloves
  2 hot peppers, seeded and chopped
  ½ tsp each of salt and ground black pepper
Pour lime mixture over steak. Cover dish or seal bag. Turn steak to coat well. Leave at room temperature for at least 30 minutes.
Place steak on barbecue and grill about 5 to 8 minutes per side for medium-rare. Remove to a platter and let stand 5 minutes before slicing diagonally.
Meanwhile, wrap in foil
  16 tortillas
  Warm in 350°F (180°C) oven for 5 minutes.
Place a warm tortilla on a plate. Spoon a row of sliced Grilled Fajita Steak down centre. Top with your favorite toppings, such as sautéed peppers, salsa, coriander, sour cream, guacamole or grated cheddar cheese. Roll up like a crêpe and enjoy.
Makes: 16 fajitas or 8 servings

PREPARATION: 10 MINUTES
MARINATE: 30 MINUTES
GRILL: 16 MINUTES

INDOOR SIZZLE:
For oven broiling, see page 10.

CAJUN STEAK

For a fiery steak, try this spicy rub and be prepared for a little smoking from the blackened steak.

Oil grill and preheat barbecue. Stir together
  2 tsp each black pepper, white pepper, paprika and dry mustard
  1 tsp each cayenne and salt
  ½ tsp each garlic powder, leaf oregano and thyme
Generously brush
  4 large steaks, such as rib eye, strip loin or porterhouse, at least 1 inch (2.5 cm) thick with
  melted butter or vegetable oil
Place steak on a plate or waxed paper and sprinkle with half the seasonings. Gently rub into both sides of steaks covering the top and sides.
Place on grill and barbecue steaks, about 5 to 8 minutes per side for medium-rare.
Makes: 4 servings

PREPARATION: 5 MINUTES
GRILL: 16 MINUTES

INDOOR SIZZLE:
For oven broiling, see page 10.

Steak & Garden-Fresh Salad

*For a new take on a steak-and-salad supper, slice sizzling steak and toss
with cool greens and a garlicky dressing.*

In a salad bowl, combine
- 1 head romaine lettuce, torn into
  bite-size pieces
- 1 sweet red pepper, chopped
- 1 ripe but firm pear, cored and thinly sliced

Refrigerate until ready to serve, up to 2 hours.

Whisk together
- ¼ cup olive oil
- ¼ cup red wine vinegar
- 2 crushed garlic gloves
- 1 tsp Dijon mustard
- ½ tsp Worcestershire sauce
- ½ tsp salt
- ½ tsp freshly ground pepper

Set aside at room temperature.

Trim fat and nick edges to prevent curling from
- 1 lb (500 g) sirloin, strip-loin or top round
  steak, at least ¾ inch (2 cm) thick

Oil grill and preheat barbecue. Grill steak about
4 to 6 minutes per side for medium-rare, then
thinly slice. Immediately toss dressing with
salad. Add warm steak slices and toss until
mixed. Serve right away.

Makes: 4 to 6 servings

PREPARATION: 25 MINUTES
GRILL: 12 MINUTES

INDOOR SIZZLE:
For oven broiling, see page 10.

STEAK & GARDEN-FRESH SALAD

BEEF

BARBECUED EYE-OF-ROUND ROAST

When serving a crowd, barbecuing a whole small roast is less stressful than tending a herd of steaks.

Oil grill and preheat barbecue. Stir together
  2 crushed garlic cloves
  1 tbsp vegetable oil
  2 tsp hot pepper sauce
Lightly brush over entire surface of
  3-lb (2.5-kg) eye-of-round
Sprinkle evenly over entire surface
  ½ tsp coarsely ground black pepper
  ½ tsp salt

If you have a meat thermometer, insert into the end of roast, deep into the centre. Place meat on grill over medium heat. Close barbecue lid or form a foil tent over roast. Barbecue, turning roast often. Check frequently and adjust temperature to low if roast is browning too quickly. For rare, grill until thermometer reads 140°F (60°C) or until meat still feels soft but is slightly springy to the touch, about 20 minutes per pound. Medium is 160°F (70°C) and well-done is 170°F (75°C).

Remove roast to a cutting board. Cover and let stand at least 5 minutes before slicing. Wonderful with grilled potatoes, peppers and tomatoes topped with basil.

Makes: 8 servings

PREPARATION: 10 MINUTES
GRILL: 1 HOUR

INDOOR SIZZLE: *Oven Roasting*
Preheat oven to 425°F (220°C).
Prepare roast and insert thermometer.
Place in a small roasting pan. Roast, uncovered, for 15 minutes. Reduce heat to 375°F (190°C) and continue roasting for 45 more minutes for medium-rare.

ULTIMATE BBQ TENDERLOIN

Here's a foolproof way for grilling tenderloin without a meat thermometer.

Measure the meat at its thickest point, then barbecue for 10 minutes per inch for rare or up to 15 minutes per inch for well-done.
Stir together
  1 tbsp cracked or coarsely ground black pepper
  1 tbsp crushed garlic, bottled or fresh
  1 tbsp Dijon or honey-Dijon mustard
Drizzle about
  1 tsp olive oil
  over
  3-lb (2.5-kg) beef tenderloin
  and rub it over the entire surface. Smear the mustard-pepper spread very thinly over the entire surface. Marinating a tenderloin to tenderize isn't necessary because it is already tender. You simply want to enhance the taste.

Oil grill and turn barbecue to high. When preheated, place meat on grill, then turn heat to medium. Close barbecue lid. Grill tenderloin, turning every 10 minutes. If tenderloin is not even in thickness, turn off one side of barbecue, then position meat so thin portion is over the turned-off side.

Place on a cutting board and cover with a tent of foil. Let stand for about 10 minutes before slicing.

Makes: 6 to 8 servings

PREPARATION: 5 MINUTES
GRILL: 30 TO 40 MINUTES

INDOOR SIZZLE:
For oven roasting, see left.

TIPS

BBQ Beef Basics

- To prevent flare-ups, trim all visible fat before grilling.
- To prevent steaks from curling, nick outside edges of steak at 2-inch (5-cm) intervals.
- To preserve juices, let a thick steak sit for 5 minutes after grilling before slicing crosswise.
- For even cooking, bring steak and roasts to room temperature before grilling.

Poking for Doneness

Instead of cutting into a steak to check how well done it is and losing precious juices, try the "poke" method instead. Press a thick steak with your finger.

- Rare steak offers a little resistance, but still feels fairly soft; takes about 5 minutes per side.
- Medium steak is a little firm, but bounces back; takes about 8 minutes per side.
- Well-done steak feels firm throughout; takes about 10 minutes per side.

Tender Steak Chart

Here's a rundown of the most popular steaks tender enough to be barbecued without marinating:

Eye-of-round: This is a moderately tender round of meat without any bones and no visible or exterior fat. Often sold with exterior coating of crushed peppercorns or seasonings.

Flank: Not a tender piece of meat, but considered acceptable when cooked medium-rare and sliced across the grain.

Porterhouse: Looks like a large T-bone steak, but the bone is smaller and the amount of meat on either side is closer in size.

Rib eye: Tender, well-marbled steak that is cut from the prime rib area. All bone has been removed from these fairly circular large steaks.

Sirloins: Cheapest of the tender cuts, sirloins are big steaks without any bones. They come from the area between the loin and the hip called the "sir-loin." Top sirloin comes from the tenderloin section and is more tender than a bottom sirloin, which comes from the hip section.

Strip loin: Very tender and boneless, these long narrow steaks are what's left when the tenderloin is removed from the loin or "stripped of the tenderloin."

T-bone: Tender and often on sale, T-bones are sliced right through the bone that holds the strip loin on one side and the tenderloin on the other.

Tenderloin: Extremely tender, these small round steaks with no bones and little fat are the most expensive. They are cut from the area directly below the loin, the part of the animal that never builds up any tough muscle. Also called filet mignons, tournedos and chateaubriands.

BURGERS

Burgers can't be beat for a satisfying comfort dinner.
This WHOPPING 3-PEPPER BURGER (see recipe page 26)
is dressed up with an adult-pleasing triple-pepper boost
and topped with grilled peppers and cheese.

THE PERFECT BASIC BURGER

*Add a gourmet-style topping (see pages 38 and 39)
and your simple supper becomes a burger event.*

In a large bowl, whisk together
  1 egg
  $\frac{1}{2}$ tsp salt
  $\frac{1}{2}$ tsp freshly ground black pepper
Add
  1 lb (500 g) ground beef
Sprinkle evenly with
  $\frac{1}{2}$ cup fine dry bread crumbs
Work with a fork or your hands until just
  blended. Overmixing toughens meat. Shape
  into 4 patties, each about ¾ inch (2 cm) thick.
Place patties on an oiled, preheated grill and
  barbecue, covered, for 6 to 8 minutes per side
  for well-done burgers.
Makes: 4 burgers

> PREPARATION: 10 MINUTES
> GRILL: 16 MINUTES

> INDOOR SIZZLE:
> *For sauté instructions, see below.*

ONION-CAPER BURGERS

*Dijon and capers add an intriguing French flavor
to these sophisticated burgers.*

In a food processor, whirl, using an on-and-off
  motion
  2 eggs
  2 small peeled onions, quartered
  $\frac{1}{2}$ cup capers, rinsed and drained
  2 tbsp Dijon mustard
  until onions are coarsely ground.
  Turn into a large bowl.
Add
  2 lbs (1 kg) ground beef
Sprinkle evenly with
  $\frac{1}{2}$ cup fine dry bread crumbs
Work with a fork or your hands until just
  blended. Overmixing toughens meat. Shape
  into 8 patties, each about ¾ inch (2 cm) thick.
Place patties on an oiled, preheated grill and
  barbecue, covered, for 6 to 8 minutes per side
  for well-done burgers.
Makes: 8 burgers

> PREPARATION: 15 MINUTES
> GRILL: 16 MINUTES

> INDOOR SIZZLE:
> *For sauté instructions, see below.*

INDOOR SAUTÉ FOR YEAR-ROUND SIZZLE

Where a recipe indicates Indoor Sizzle, prepare burgers as directed, but when it's time to barbecue, use this stove-top method instead. Lightly coat a large frying pan with oil. Set over medium heat. Add burgers. Do not crowd pan. Sauté, uncovered, for about 6 to 8 minutes per side for well-done burgers. (Beef burgers should always be well-done.) If burgers brown too quickly, reduce heat to medium-low. Repeat with remaining burgers.

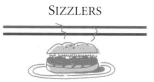

SPEEDY SPICY MEXICAN BURGERS

*These burgers are a snap to make. Shape into ovals, grill and then bundle
into warm tortillas and heap with lots of toppings.*

Place in a large bowl
   1 lb (500 g) ground beef
Sprinkle with
   1 small onion, finely chopped
   2 tsp Worcestershire sauce
   2 tsp chili powder
   ½ tsp leaf oregano
   ½ tsp cumin
   ½ tsp garlic powder
   ¼ tsp hot pepper sauce
Work with a fork or your hands until just
   blended. Overmixing toughens meat. Shape
   into 4 patties, each about ¾ inch (2 cm) thick.

Place patties on an oiled, preheated grill and
   barbecue, covered, for 6 to 8 minutes per side
   for well-done burgers. Place burgers on rolls
   or tortillas. Dress with sour cream, sliced
   onions and slivered hot peppers.
Makes: 4 burgers

PREPARATION: 10 MINUTES
GRILL: 16 MINUTES

INDOOR SIZZLE:
For sauté instructions, see page 24.

SPEEDY SPICY MEXICAN BURGERS

BURGERS

WHOPPING 3-PEPPER BURGER

Adding a mix of coarsely ground colorful peppercorns to burgers raises them to new heights.

In a large bowl, whisk together
  1 egg
  1 tsp coarsely ground pepper, preferably a
    mix of black, white, red and green
    peppercorns
  ½ tsp salt
Add
  1 lb (500 g) ground beef or veal
Sprinkle evenly with
  ¼ cup fine dry bread crumbs
Work with a fork or your hands until just
  blended. Overmixing toughens meat. Shape
  into 4 patties, each about ¾ inch (2 cm) thick.
Place patties on an oiled, preheated grill and
  barbecue, covered, for 6 to 8 minutes per side
  for well-done burgers.
For cheeseburgers, top patties about 4 minutes
  before burgers are done with
  a slice of full-flavored cheese such as
    aged cheddar, Asiago or Fontina, or a
    crumbling of Stilton or goat's cheese
Makes: 4 burgers

PREPARATION: 10 MINUTES
GRILL: 16 MINUTES

OLD-FASHIONED CHILI BURGERS

Classic chili sauce mixed into the burger keeps it juicy and basil adds a fresh-flavor wallop.

In a large bowl, whisk together
  1 egg
  ¼ cup chili sauce or hot salsa
  ¼ cup finely chopped fresh basil
    or 1 tsp dried basil
  ¼ tsp hot pepper sauce
  ¼ tsp salt
  freshly ground black pepper
Add
  1 lb (500 g) ground beef
Sprinkle evenly with
  ¼ cup fine dry bread crumbs
Work with a fork or your hands until just
  blended. Overmixing toughens meat. Shape
  into 4 patties, each about ¾ inch (2 cm) thick.
Place patties on an oiled, preheated grill and
  barbecue, covered, for 6 to 8 minutes per side
  for well-done burgers. Serve on a sesame bun
  with sliced tomatoes.
Makes: 4 burgers

PREPARATION: 10 MINUTES
GRILL: 16 MINUTES

INDOOR SIZZLE:
For sauté instructions, see page 24.

Whopping 3-Pepper Burger

CHÈVRE-FILLED BURGERS

Here's an easy way to add class and a delightful flavor twist to burgers.

In a large bowl, whisk together
  finely grated peel of 1 lemon
  1 egg
  ¼ cup chopped fresh dill
  ½ tsp salt
  ½ tsp freshly ground black pepper
Add and blend
  1 lb (500 g) ground beef,
    veal or chicken
Slice into 4 pieces
  2 oz (60 g) goat's cheese,
    preferably semi-firm
On waxed paper, shape cheese into thin rounds about 1½ inches (4 cm) in diameter.
Divide meat into 8 pieces. Form each into a thin patty, about 3½ inches (9 cm) wide. Sandwich 1 cheese round between 2 meat patties and seal edges well around cheese. Burgers can be made up to 8 hours ahead, covered with plastic wrap and refrigerated.
Place patties on an oiled, preheated grill and barbecue, covered, for 6 to 8 minutes per side for well-done burgers. Serve on crusty rolls spread with mayonnaise or Dijon mustard. While grilling, don't press or prick burgers or the cheese filling will ooze out.
Makes: 4 burgers

PREPARATION: 20 MINUTES
GRILL: 16 MINUTES

GREEK FETA BURGERS

For a truly outstanding burger, mix creamy feta and seasonings into burgers before grilling.

In a large bowl, whisk together
  1 egg
  ½ to ¾ tsp Italian seasoning
  ¼ tsp salt
  freshly ground black pepper
Crumble in
  ¾ cup feta cheese
Add
  1 lb (500 g) ground beef, veal or lamb
Sprinkle evenly with
  ¼ cup fine dry bread crumbs
Work with a fork or your hands until just blended. Overmixing toughens meat. Shape into 4 patties, each about ¾ inch (2 cm) thick.
Place patties on an oiled, preheated grill and barbecue, covered, for 6 to 8 minutes per side for well-done burgers. Serve on crusty rolls spread with Dijon mustard and topped with slices of juicy tomatoes.
Makes: 4 burgers

PREPARATION: 10 MINUTES
GRILL: 16 MINUTES

INDOOR SIZZLE:
For sauté instructions, see page 24.

Chèvre-Filled Burgers

BURGERS

JAZZED-UP ONION BURGERS

A few dashes of steak sauce and sweet onions create an incredibly robust burger.

In a large bowl, whisk together
  1 egg
  1 tsp Worcestershire sauce
  1/2 tsp hot pepper sauce
  1/2 tsp salt
  1/4 tsp freshly ground black pepper
Add
  1 lb (500 g) ground beef
and sprinkle with
  1/2 cup finely chopped sweet white
    onion, such as Vidalia or Bermuda
  1 large crushed garlic clove
  2 tbsp chopped fresh parsley
Work with a fork or your hands until just
  blended. Overmixing toughens meat. Shape
  into 4 patties, each about 3/4 inch (2 cm) thick.
Place patties on an oiled, preheated grill and
  barbecue, covered, for 6 to 8 minutes per side
  for well-done burgers. Serve on fresh kaiser
  rolls topped with lettuce, tomato, thin slices
  of onion and salsa sauce.
Makes: 4 burgers

PREPARATION: 10 MINUTES
GRILL: 16 MINUTES

INDOOR SIZZLE:
For sauté instructions, see page 24.

EASY CAESAR BURGERS

Mix a burger with all the great ingredients that create a superb creamy Caesar dressing.

In a large bowl, whisk together
  1 egg
  1/4 cup creamy Caesar dressing
Stir in
  1/4 cup grated Parmesan cheese
  1 slice bread, crumbled
  1 slice crumbled cooked bacon or
    1 tbsp bacon bits
  1 large crushed garlic clove
  1/2 tsp freshly ground black pepper
Add
  1 lb (500 g) ground beef
Work with a fork or your hands until just
  blended. Overmixing toughens meat. Shape
  into 4 patties, each about 3/4 inch (2 cm) thick.
Place patties on an oiled, preheated grill and
  barbecue, covered, for 6 to 8 minutes per side
  for well-done burgers. Serve on crusty rolls
  with bacon strips, sliced tomatoes, shredded
  Romaine and a big dollop of Caesar dressing.
Makes: 4 burgers

PREPARATION: 10 MINUTES
GRILL: 16 MINUTES

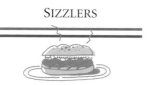

New Salsa Cheeseburgers

Jazz up ground beef with spicy salsa and whatever cheese you have on hand.
Serve on fresh kaiser rolls topped with fiery salsa, nippy cheddar or guacamole.

Whisk together
  1 egg
  ¼ cup salsa
  ½ tsp cumin
  ½ tsp salt
  ¼ tsp cayenne pepper
  ¼ tsp black pepper
Stir in
  ¼ cup fine dry bread crumbs
Add
  1 lb (500 g) ground beef
  and blend, using a fork or your hands.
Work in
  ½ cup grated cheddar,
    Fontina or Asiago cheese

Work with a fork or your hands until just
  blended. Overmixing toughens meat. Shape
  into 4 patties, each about ¾ inch (2 cm) thick.
Place patties on an oiled, preheated grill and
  barbecue, covered, for 6 to 8 minutes per side
  for well-done burgers.
Makes: 4 burgers

PREPARATION: 10 MINUTES
GRILL: 16 MINUTES

INDOOR SIZZLE:
For sauté instructions, see page 24.

New Salsa Cheeseburgers

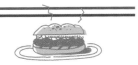

BURGERS

MINT & CUMIN BURGERS

*Slip these cumin-scented patties into pita bread
and drizzle with Jalapeño-Yogurt Sauce.*

In a large bowl, whisk
    1 egg
Add
    1 lb (500 g) ground beef or lamb
    1 bunch fresh mint, chopped
        (about ⅓ cup)
    1 onion, finely chopped
    2 crushed garlic cloves
    1 tsp ground cumin
    ½ tsp salt
    ¼ tsp cayenne pepper
Work with a fork or your hands until just blended.
    Overmixing toughens meat. Shape into 4
    patties, each about ¾ inch (2 cm) thick.
Place patties on an oiled, preheated grill and
    barbecue, covered, for 6 to 8 minutes per side
    for well-done burgers. Meanwhile, prepare
    Jalapeño-Yogurt Sauce (see recipe below).
    Serve burgers in pita bread with shredded
    lettuce and Jalapeño-Yogurt Sauce.
Makes: 4 burgers

> *PREPARATION: 10 MINUTES*
> *GRILL: 16 MINUTES*

INDOOR SIZZLE:
For sauté instructions, see page 24.

JALAPEÑO-YOGURT SAUCE

Stir together
    ½ cup thick yogurt or
        light sour cream
    1 jalapeño pepper, seeded and
        finely chopped
    1 tbsp freshly squeezed lemon juice
    ¼ tsp salt

SPICY MIDDLE EASTERN BURGERS

*Spiced with cumin, coriander, cayenne and parsley,
a Mediterranean kefta mixture has intriguing flavor.*

Place in a large bowl
    1 lb (500 g) ground beef or lamb
        or a mixture of both
Sprinkle evenly with
    1 onion, very finely chopped
    ½ cup finely chopped fresh parsley
    1 tsp ground cumin
    ½ tsp ground coriander
    ½ tsp paprika
    ½ tsp salt
    ¼ tsp cayenne pepper
Add
    1 egg, beaten
Blend mixture until ingredients are evenly
    distributed. Divide meat into 8 pieces and
    shape into oblong patties, each about ½ inch
    (1 cm) thick.
Place patties on an oiled, preheated grill and
    barbecue, covered, for 6 to 8 minutes per side
    for well-done burgers.
Warm
    4 pitas
    on grill, about 1 minute per side,
    then slice one end open.
Stuff 2 patties into each pita and top with
    shredded lettuce, tomato, chopped cucumber
    and a dollop of tzatziki.
Makes: 8 oblong patties for 4 servings

> *PREPARATION: 15 MINUTES*
> *GRILL: 16 MINUTES*

FRENCH LAMB BURGERS

For a sophisticated appetizer at your next barbecue party, form these burgers into small patties, grill and serve in mini pitas.

In a large bowl, whisk together
  1 egg
  1 tbsp Dijon mustard
  2 tsp dried tarragon
  ¼ tsp freshly ground black or
    white pepper
Add
  1 lb (500 g) ground lamb or chicken
Work with a fork or your hands until just blended. Overmixing toughens meat. Shape into 4 patties, each about ¾ inch (2 cm) thick or about 12 mini patties, about 1½ inches (4 cm) wide.

Place patties on an oiled, preheated grill and barbecue, covered, for 4 to 8 minutes per side for well-done burgers. Serve in warmed regular or mini pita bread topped with chopped tomatoes and a dab of sour cream. Serve with grilled corn.

Makes: 4 burgers or 12 appetizers

PREPARATION: 10 MINUTES
GRILL: 16 MINUTES

FRENCH LAMB BURGERS

HOT SAUSAGE BURGERS

For fans of Italian sausage, this burger has all the taste with very little work.

In a large bowl, whisk together
    1 egg
    2 tsp Dijon or hot mustard
    1 crushed garlic clove
    ½ tsp dried oregano
    ½ tsp dried basil
    ¼ tsp hot red pepper flakes (optional)
Add
    ½ lb (250 g) hot Italian sausage,
       casings removed
    ½ lb (250 g) ground pork or beef
    Sprinkle evenly with
    ¼ cup fine dry bread crumbs
Work with a fork or your hands until just blended. Overmixing toughens meat. Shape into 6 patties, each about ½ inch (1 cm) thick.
Place burgers on an oiled, preheated barbecue. Cover and grill for 5 to 7 minutes per side. Serve on crusty rolls.
Makes: 6 burgers

PREPARATION: 15 MINUTES
GRILL: 14 MINUTES

INDOOR SIZZLE:
For sauté instructions, see page 24.

CURRIED BURGERS

Punch up burgers with curry and pepper flakes. Then lavishly spread with sour cream and chutney.

In a large bowl, stir together
    1 egg
    1 onion, very finely chopped
    1 tsp curry powder
    ½ tsp hot red pepper flakes
    ½ tsp salt
Add
    1 lb (500 g) ground lamb, chicken or pork
Sprinkle evenly with
    ¼ cup fine dry bread crumbs
Work with a fork or your hands until just blended. Overmixing toughens meat. Shape into 4 patties, each about ¾ inch (2 cm) thick.
Place patties on an oiled, preheated grill and barbecue, covered, for 6 to 8 minutes per side for well-done burgers.
Makes: 4 burgers

PREPARATION: 10 MINUTES
GRILL: 16 MINUTES

INDOOR SIZZLE:
For sauté instructions, see page 24.

Curried Burgers

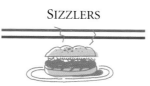

CHICKEN BURGERS ITALIANO

These chicken burgers are incredibly moist, with a rich sophisticated taste.

In a large bowl, whisk together
   ¼ cup freshly grated Parmesan
   1 egg
   ½ tsp Italian seasoning
   1 crushed garlic clove
   ¼ tsp salt
Add
   1 lb (500 g) ground chicken or turkey
   and work mixture with a fork or your fingers
   until combined. Form into 4 patties, each
   about ¾ inch (2 cm) thick.
Place burgers on an oiled, preheated grill and
   barbecue, covered, for 8 minutes per side.
   Serve in warm pitas or crusty buns and
   spoon chopped tomatoes and avocados or
   salsa over top.
Makes: 4 burgers

PREPARATION: 10 MINUTES
GRILL: 16 MINUTES

INDOOR SIZZLE:
For sauté instructions, see page 24.

SAGE-ORANGE CHICKEN BURGERS

Inexpensive ground chicken gets sophistication with the addition of finely grated orange peel and sage.

Combine
   1 lb (500 g) ground chicken or turkey
   finely grated peel of ½ orange
   1 tbsp Dijon mustard
   ½ tsp dried rubbed sage or
      ¼ tsp ground sage
   ½ tsp salt
   ¼ tsp cayenne or black pepper
   (optional)
Work with a fork or your hands until just
   blended. Overmixing toughens meat. Shape
   into 4 patties, each about ¾ inch (2 cm) thick.
Place patties on an oiled, preheated grill and
   barbecue, covered, for 8 minutes per side for
   well-done burgers.
Makes: 4 burgers

PREPARATION: 10 MINUTES
GRILL: 16 MINUTES

INDOOR SIZZLE:
For sauté instructions, see page 24.

Chicken Burgers Italiano

SAGE 'N' THYME BURGERS

Sage, thyme and lemon zest mixed with ground pork or veal tastes absolutely divine.

In a large bowl, whisk together
- 1 egg
- 2 whole green onions,
  very finely chopped
- finely grated peel of 1 lemon
- ½ tsp leaf sage
- ½ tsp leaf thyme
- ½ tsp salt
- ½ tsp freshly ground black pepper

Add
- 1 lb (500 g) ground veal, chicken
  or pork

Sprinkle evenly with
- ¼ cup fine dry bread crumbs

Work with a fork or your hands until just blended. Overmixing toughens meat. Shape into 4 patties, each about ¾ inch (2 cm) thick.

Place patties on an oiled, preheated grill and barbecue, covered, for 6 to 8 minutes per side for well-done burgers. Serve immediately on kaiser buns spread with mustard. Grilled apple slices also go well with these burgers.

Makes: 4 burgers

PREPARATION: 10 MINUTES
GRILL: 16 MINUTES

PARMIGIANA VEAL BURGERS

Grated Parmigiana Reggiana keeps these burgers moist without overpowering veal's delicate taste.

In a large bowl, whisk together
- 1 egg
- ½ cup grated Parmesan cheese
- ¼ cup chopped fresh basil
  or 1 tsp dried basil
- 1 crushed garlic clove
- ½ tsp salt
- ¼ tsp freshly ground black pepper

Add
- 1 lb (500 g) ground veal or chicken

Work with a fork or your hands until just blended. Overmixing toughens meat. Shape into 4 patties, each about ¾ inch (2 cm) thick.

Place patties on an oiled, preheated grill and barbecue, covered, for 6 to 8 minutes per side for well-done burgers. Serve with mashed potatoes and a dilled cucumber salad or on soft rolls topped with light sour cream and sliced tomatoes.

Makes: 4 burgers

PREPARATION: 10 MINUTES
GRILL: 16 MINUTES

INDOOR SIZZLE:
For sauté instructions, see page 24.

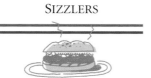

DOUBLE-PUNCH BBQ BURGERS

The double whammy of barbecue flavor comes from stirring sauce into burgers, then basting generously while grilling.

Whisk together
  1 egg
  ¼ cup barbecue sauce, regular or
    smoky-flavored
Crumble into mixture
  1 lb (500 g) ground beef or veal
  and sprinkle with
  ¼ cup fine dry bread crumbs
  ½ tsp coarsely ground black pepper
  ¼ tsp cayenne pepper (optional)

Work with a fork or your hands until just blended. Overmixing toughens meat. Shape into 4 patties, each about ¾ inch (2 cm) thick.

Place patties on an oiled, preheated grill and barbecue, covered, for 6 to 8 minutes per side for well-done burgers, basting with a little barbecue sauce after turning. Tuck into buns and top with lettuce and sliced onions.

Makes: 4 burgers

> *PREPARATION: 10 MINUTES*
> *GRILL: 16 MINUTES*

DOUBLE-PUNCH BBQ BURGERS

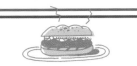

BURGERS

LIGHT CREAMY VEAL BURGERS

Serve these delicately flavored and sophisticated burgers with mashed potatoes and grilled peppers.

In a large bowl, whisk together
  1 egg
  ¼ cup sour cream
  1 tsp Dijon mustard
  1 crushed garlic clove
  ¼ tsp salt
  ¼ tsp dried tarragon
  freshly ground black pepper
Add
  1 lb (500 g) ground veal, beef
    or chicken
Sprinkle evenly with
  ¼ cup fine dry bread crumbs
Work with a fork or your hands until just
  blended. Overmixing toughens meat. Shape
  into 4 patties, each about ¾ inch (2 cm) thick.
Place patties on an oiled, preheated grill and
  barbecue, covered, for 6 to 8 minutes per side
  for well-done burgers.
  Makes: 4 burgers

> PREPARATION: 10 MINUTES
> GRILL: 16 MINUTES

INDOOR SIZZLE:
For sauté instructions, see page 24.

PORK BURGERS WITH SAGE

This is the burger to flip when you're feeling like something substantial, but not too heavy.

In a large bowl, whisk together
  1 egg
  finely grated peel of 1 orange
  2 tbsp finely chopped fresh sage
    or 1 tsp dried sage
  ¼ tsp dry mustard
  ½ tsp salt
  freshly ground black pepper
    or generous pinch of cayenne pepper
Sprinkle evenly with
  ¼ cup fine dry bread crumbs
Add
  1 lb (500 g) ground pork
Work with a fork or your hands until just
  blended. Overmixing toughens meat. Shape
  into 4 patties, each about ¾ inch (2 cm) thick.
Place patties on an oiled, preheated grill and
  barbecue, covered, for 6 to 8 minutes per side
  for well-done burgers. Serve pork patties with
  a sauce made by blending a little sour cream
  with Dijon mustard. Serve with a crisp
  coleslaw and grilled apple slices.
  Makes: 4 burgers

> PREPARATION: 10 MINUTES
> GRILL: 16 MINUTES

INDOOR SIZZLE:
For sauté instructions, see page 24.

TIPS

BBQ Burger Basics

- Oil grill before turning on the barbecue or food will stick and burgers may fall apart.

- Use medium or regular ground beef. Lean beef tends to fall apart. Stir in an egg and up to ½ cup dry or fresh bread crumbs.

- Make hamburgers just before grilling. Beef burgers start losing their bright red color within an hour or two of preparation.

- Use your hands to lightly mix ground beef. Overhandling toughens meat. You can wear thin plastic gloves to prevent meat from getting tacky. Always wash hands thoroughly after forming burger.

- Be gentle during cooking. Rough play (poking or batting down with a spatula) squeezes out precious juices.

- Always cook beef burgers until well-done to kill all bacteria. Most will need about 6 to 8 minutes per side on the barbecue. Never eat them rare.

- Vary your meats. Most burger recipes will work with ground chicken, veal and pork as well as beef or a combination of meats. A little hot Italian sausage added to ground beef adds a wallop of taste.

Burger Perk-Ups

Toppings aren't the only flavor brighteners.
Mix into ground meat any of the following:

- drained salsa sauce and grated cheddar
- puréed fresh ginger, garlic and chopped sweet or green onions
- garlic roasted in its own skin until soft, then mashed with a fork
- chopped fresh basil and crumbled goat's cheese or feta
- Parmesan, oregano and garlic
- chutney, curry powder and sour cream
- grated smoked Gouda and chopped fresh dill
- hot red pepper flakes, chopped jalapeños or pickled hot peppers

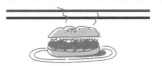

QUICK BURGER TOPPINGS

THREE-PEPPER RELISH

Serve this easy relish hot or cold. If not using right away, store in a sealed jar in the refrigerator.

Seed and finely chop
   1 small sweet red pepper
   1 small sweet green pepper
   1 small sweet yellow pepper
In a large wide frying pan, heat
   2 tbsp olive or vegetable oil
Add chopped peppers and
   2 garlic cloves, finely chopped
Cook over medium heat, stirring frequently, for about 5 minutes or just until peppers are softened. Remove from heat. Taste and season with salt and pepper.
Makes: 1 cup

PREPARATION: 15 MINUTES
COOK: 5 MINUTES

ISLAND CHUTNEY

Sauce can be served hot or cold. If not using right away, store in a sealed jar in the refrigerator.

In a medium-size frying pan, combine
   1 cup chopped fresh pineapple
      and any juice that may have collected
   3 tbsp of your favorite chutney
   1 tbsp chopped pimento
   $\frac{1}{4}$ tsp curry powder
Place over medium heat, stirring frequently, until pineapple is slightly softened and completely coated with sauce, for 3 to 4 minutes. Excellent over chicken or veal burgers.
Makes: 1 cup

PREPARATION: 10 MINUTES
COOK: 4 MINUTES

CALIFORNIA AVOCADO CHILI

Creamy avocado makes a superb topper, especially for chicken burgers.

Peel and slice into bite-size pieces
   1 ripe avocado
Stir together and add to avocado
   $\frac{1}{4}$ cup sour cream
   $\frac{1}{2}$ tsp lime juice
   pinch of hot red pepper flakes
      or cayenne pepper
Taste and add more lime juice, hot red pepper flakes and salt and pepper if needed. It's best to make this topping just before serving, as the avocado may darken after cutting.
Makes: ½ cup

PREPARATION: 5 MINUTES

LIGHT HORSERADISH BURGER SAUCE

A hit of horseradish gives a wake-up call to any burger.

Stir together
   $\frac{1}{4}$ cup ketchup
   2 tbsp prepared horseradish
   1 tsp Worcestershire sauce
   dash of hot pepper sauce
   pinches of salt and freshly ground
      black pepper
Use immediately or refrigerate, covered, until ready to serve. It will keep well for weeks.
Makes: ⅓ cup

PREPARATION: 5 MINUTES

BURGERS

38

TOMATO, BACON & ROQUEFORT

Want to add a wallop of class to any burger? Simply top with this winning trio of taste combos.

In a large frying pan, cook until crisp
    4 slices bacon
    Remove and drain on paper towel. Break or slice into bite-size pieces.
Stir bacon with
    2 tomatoes, seeded and coarsely chopped
    1/4 cup crumbled Roquefort or blue cheese
    1/4 tsp freshly ground black pepper
If not using right away, refrigerate. Tomatoes will start to soften after 2 or 3 hours.
    Makes: 1/2 cup

    PREPARATION: 10 MINUTES
    COOK: 4 MINUTES

ORIENTAL SAUCE

Drizzle over burgers and serve on a bed of rice along with BBQ Sweet Peppers (see recipe page 124).

In a small saucepan, bring to a boil, stirring often
    1/4 cup soy sauce
    3 tbsp orange juice concentrate
    2 green onions, finely chopped
    1/4 tsp ground ginger
In a small bowl, blend
    1 tsp cornstarch
    1 tbsp water
Stir into soy mixture as soon as it comes to a boil. Stir gently over medium heat until slightly thickened, about 3 minutes. Cool to room temperature. Use right away or refrigerate, covered, until ready to use. It will keep well for several days.
    Makes: 1/3 cup

    PREPARATION: 10 MINUTES
    COOK: 5 MINUTES

GREAT GREEK TOPPER

Lavishly spread this herbed creamy feta over hot burgers and serve with sliced tomatoes.

In a medium-size bowl, whisk together
    3 tbsp olive oil
    1/2 tsp dried rosemary
    freshly ground black pepper
Crumble in
    1/2 cup feta cheese
Stir gently with a fork until evenly blended. Lavishly spread over hot burgers or cover and refrigerate until ready to serve. It will keep well for 2 to 3 days.
    Makes: 3/4 cup

    PREPARATION: 5 MINUTES

BURGER SALSA

Nothing beats the flavor of a freshly made salsa. Great as a topper for any burger.

Whisk together
    2 to 3 tbsp olive oil
    1 tbsp red wine vinegar
    2 tbsp finely chopped Italian parsley
    1 tbsp finely chopped jalapeño pepper
    1 crushed garlic clove
    pinches of salt and freshly ground black pepper
Stir in
    2 tomatoes, seeded and cut into 1/4-inch (0.5-cm) pieces
    2 green onions, thinly sliced
    1/2 small green pepper, diced
Let stand, covered, at room temperature for an hour. Use right away or refrigerate until ready to serve.
    Makes: 2 cups

    PREPARATION: 10 MINUTES

CHICKEN

The picture-perfect take-off on a Caribbean classic,
this GRILLED JERK CHICKEN (see recipe page 48) couldn't
be easier. Slather aromatic allspice, chili peppers
and thyme over chicken breasts and grill to moist perfection.
Serve on island-style rice and beans.

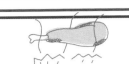

CHICKEN

GRILLED FIVE-HERB CHICKEN

Add a mix of herbs to your next chicken grill for an exciting dressed-up flavor.

Oil grill and preheat barbecue. Whisk together
    1/4 cup olive or vegetable oil
    2 tbsp freshly squeezed lemon juice
    1 tsp granulated sugar
    1/2 tsp dried tarragon
    1/2 tsp dillweed
    1/2 tsp dried basil
    1/4 tsp dried leaf oregano
    1/4 tsp savory
Place
    4 skinned chicken breasts or legs
    on 4 pieces of foil large enough to securely
    wrap. Brush with herb mixture. Save
    remaining mixture. Seal foil and place
    packets on grill. Grill for 30 minutes, turning
    partway through.
Remove chicken from foil and discard juices.
    Place chicken directly on grill. Brush with
    saved herb mixture. Grill chicken for 5 to 10
    minutes per side, turning often and brushing
    with herb mixture until chicken feels springy.
Makes: 4 servings

PREPARATION: 5 MINUTES
GRILL: 50 MINUTES

INDOOR SIZZLE:
For oven roasting, see below.

GINGER-LIME YOGURT CHICKEN

Quickly grill chicken, then lavishly cover with a sumptuous yogurt sauce. Good with couscous.

Oil grill and preheat barbecue.
Brush
    4 skinless, boneless chicken breasts
    with
    olive, sesame or vegetable oil
    Then season lightly with
    salt
    white pepper
Place on grill. Barbecue, turning once, until
    chicken feels springy, about 15 minutes.
Meanwhile, stir together
    2/3 cup yogurt
    1 tbsp freshly grated ginger
    finely grated peel of 1 lime
    1 tbsp freshly squeezed lime juice
Taste and add a pinch of sugar if you prefer a less
    tart taste. When chicken is grilled, place on
    individual plates and spoon sauce over top.
Makes: 4 servings

PREPARATION: 10 MINUTES
GRILL: 15 MINUTES

INDOOR ROASTING FOR YEAR-ROUND SIZZLE

Where a recipe indicates Indoor Sizzle, prepare chicken as directed, but when it's time to barbecue, use this oven method instead. Preheat oven to 375°F (190°C). Brush chicken liberally with mixture. Place on a rack set in a shallow baking pan. Roast, uncovered, in preheated oven for 45 to 55 minutes for breasts or legs and 35 to 40 minutes for thighs, basting often with the mixture. If chicken browns before the end of the cooking time, cover loosely with a piece of foil to prevent burning.

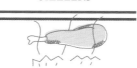

BBQ Honey & Thyme Chicken

You probably have all the ingredients on hand to dress up chicken with this complementary combo of flavors. And the baste is a snap to stir together.

Place
  4 skinless, boneless chicken breasts
  in a dish just large enough to hold them or in
  a large self-sealing bag.
Stir together
  finely grated peel and juice of 1 lemon
  2 tbsp olive or vegetable oil
  1 tbsp liquid honey
  2 large crushed garlic cloves
  ½ tsp ground thyme
  generous pinches of salt and black pepper

Pour over chicken and leave at room
  temperature for about 15 minutes or
  refrigerate for several hours.
Oil grill and preheat barbecue. Remove
  chicken from marinade and place on grill.
  Barbecue until chicken feels springy,
  about 5 to 8 minutes per side. Serve with
  grilled zucchini.
Makes: 4 servings

> *PREPARATION: 10 MINUTES*
> *MARINATE: 15 MINUTES*
> *GRILL: 16 MINUTES*

BBQ HONEY & THYME CHICKEN

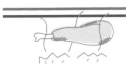

GREEK LEMON CHICKEN

A luxurious bath of olive oil, lemon juice and garlic creates an incredibly moist chicken.

In a bowl or self-sealing bag, whisk or shake
together
   3 tbsp olive oil
   finely grated peel and juice of 1 lemon
   2 crushed garlic cloves
      or 1 tsp bottled minced garlic
   ½ tsp dried leaf oregano
   ¼ tsp cracked black pepper
Add and turn until well coated
   4 skinless, boneless chicken breasts
   Cover bowl or seal bag. Refrigerate for at least
   1 hour or 3 to 4 hours.
Oil grill and preheat barbecue. Remove chicken
   from marinade and place on grill. Barbecue
   for 6 minutes, until chicken feels firm. Turn
   chicken and barbecue for 6 to 10 more
   minutes. Garnish with freshly grated lemon
   peel and fresh sprigs of oregano if you wish.
   Serve with a big Greek salad.
Makes: 4 servings

PREPARATION: 5 MINUTES
MARINATE: 1 HOUR
GRILL: 16 MINUTES

BBQ CHICKEN FINGERS

A kid-pleasing Oriental sauce replaces the usual breading on these lean fingers.

Cut lengthwise into 1-inch (2.5-cm) strips
   4 skinless, boneless chicken breasts,
      about 1 lb (500 g)
Stir together
   ½ cup plum sauce
   2 tbsp soy sauce
   ½ tsp prepared mustard

Oil grill and preheat barbecue to medium. Brush
   chicken strips with
   1 tbsp sesame oil, preferably dark
   then plum sauce mixture, and place on grill.
   Grill, turning chicken frequently and
   brushing with additional sauce, until strips
   feel springy and are richly glazed, about 10 to
   12 minutes. Serve with Fresh Mint &
   Nectarine Salsa (see recipe page 108).
Makes: 4 servings

PREPARATION: 5 MINUTES
GRILL: 12 MINUTES

FIERY GRILLED CHICKEN

Spunky salsa sauce and white wine add a marvelous spark of taste to chicken breasts.

Stir together
   ⅓ cup store-bought salsa
      or Salsa Italiano (see recipe page 114)
   ⅓ cup white wine
   3 tbsp olive oil
   3 crushed garlic cloves
Place
   6 skinless, boneless chicken breasts
   in a shallow glass dish, such as a 9-inch
   (23-cm) baking pan or pie plate. Add mixture
   and turn once or twice, coating both sides.
Cover and refrigerate for at least 1 hour or
   overnight, turning partway through.
Oil grill and preheat barbecue. Remove chicken
   from marinade and place on grill. Barbecue
   until chicken feels springy, about 5 to
   8 minutes per side.
Makes: 6 servings

PREPARATION: 5 MINUTES
MARINATE: 1 HOUR
GRILL: 16 MINUTES

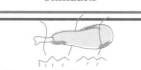

HOISIN CHICKEN

Our barbecue technique is fuss-free, and there's no fear of burned or underdone chicken.
Serve with grilled vegetables, such as peppers and zucchini.

Oil grill and preheat barbecue.
Remove skin from
  4 chicken breasts or legs
Place each chicken part on a piece of heavy foil
  large enough to securely wrap it.
Stir together
  $\frac{1}{2}$ cup hoisin sauce
  2 tbsp ketchup
  2 tbsp soy sauce
  2 tbsp freshly squeezed lemon juice
  2 crushed garlic cloves
Spoon about 2 tbsp of sauce over each piece of
  chicken. Bring long edges of foil together, fold
  over several times and seal ends. Press foil
  down to form a flat packet.

Place packets on grill and barbecue for
  45 minutes, turning 2 or 3 times. Then
  remove packets from grill. Open and discard
  juices.
Place chicken on grill. Barbecue, turning
  and basting with hoisin mixture, until
  golden brown and richly glazed, about
  5 to 7 minutes. Watch carefully to avoid
  burning. Use any remaining hoisin mixture
  as a dipping sauce.
Makes: 4 servings

PREPARATION: 5 MINUTES
GRILL: 50 MINUTES

HOISIN CHICKEN

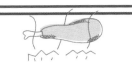

CHICKEN

GARLIC HERBED CHICKEN

For moist chicken, begin cooking in foil packets. Then finish chicken right on the grill.

Oil grill and preheat barbecue. Whisk together
    1/2 cup olive or vegetable oil
    6 large crushed garlic cloves
    2 tsp dried tarragon
    1/2 tsp freshly ground black or white pepper
    1/2 tsp salt
Place
    4 large skinned chicken breasts or legs
on 4 pieces of foil large enough to securely wrap. Brush chicken liberally with garlic-herb mixture. Save remaining mixture. Seal foil and place packets on grill and barbecue for 40 minutes, turning often.
Remove packets from grill. Carefully open and discard juices. Place chicken on greased grill. Brush with remaining garlic-herb mixture. Grill chicken for 5 to 10 minutes per side, turning often and brushing with garlic-herb mixture until chicken feels springy.
Makes: 4 servings

> *PREPARATION: 5 MINUTES*
> *GRILL: 1 HOUR*

INDOOR SIZZLE:
For oven roasting, see page 42.

EASY CURRY CHICKEN

Foil packets filled with curry and orange concentrate create a dandy bath for chicken.

Oil grill and preheat barbecue. Whisk together
    1/2 cup frozen orange juice concentrate
    1/3 cup vegetable oil
    2 tbsp curry powder
    1 tsp garlic salt
Place
    4 skinned chicken breasts or drumsticks,
        about 1 1/2 lbs (750 g)
on 4 pieces of foil large enough to securely wrap. Brush chicken with curry-orange mixture. Save remaining mixture. Seal foil and place packets on grill and barbecue for 30 minutes, turning often.
Remove chicken from foil and discard juices. Place chicken directly on greased grill. Brush with remaining curry-orange mixture. Grill chicken for 10 to 15 minutes per side, turning often and brushing with curry-orange mixture until chicken feels springy. Use remaining mixture as a dipping sauce.
Makes: 4 servings

> *PREPARATION: 5 MINUTES*
> *GRILL: 1 HOUR*

INDOOR SIZZLE:
For oven roasting, see page 42.

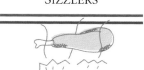

CHILI CHICKEN

This chicken packs a punch. Serve with cold beer and potato salad.

Oil grill and preheat barbecue to low. Stir together
  ⅓ cup frozen orange juice concentrate
  2 tbsp liquid honey
  2 tbsp soy sauce
  1 tsp chili powder
  1 crushed garlic clove
  generous pinch of cayenne (optional)

Place, bone-side down on barbecue, over low heat, skinning if you wish
  6 chicken pieces, such as legs, breasts or thighs, about 3 lbs (1.5 kg)

Grill slowly with lid closed, turning often until almost done, about 40 minutes. Then brush frequently with orange-honey mixture until glazed and chicken feels springy, about 10 to 20 more minutes. Remove chicken to a platter and pour any remaining orange-honey mixture over top.

Makes: 6 to 8 servings

PREPARATION: 10 MINUTES
GRILL: 1 HOUR

RASPBERRY CHICKEN

For an elegant taste that doesn't break the bank, invest in a bottle of raspberry vinegar.

Oil grill and preheat barbecue. Whisk together
  ¼ cup olive oil
  3 tbsp raspberry vinegar
  2 tbsp finely chopped fresh mint
    or 1 tsp dried mint
  ½ tsp freshly ground black pepper

Immerse
  4 skinless, boneless chicken breasts

1 piece at a time, in raspberry mixture, then place on grill. Grill, turning and basting frequently with oil mixture, until chicken feels springy, about 10 to 15 minutes. Remove chicken from grill and immediately drizzle with any remaining mixture.

Makes: 4 servings

PREPARATION: 5 MINUTES
GRILL: 15 MINUTES

Raspberry Chicken

47

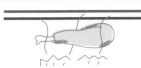

CHICKEN

GRILLED JERK CHICKEN

Serve these sensational fiery-hot chicken breasts over rice and beans.

In a food processor, whirl until fairly smooth
   4 jalapeño or hot peppers, seeded
   1 small onion, cut into quarters
   Add
   1/4 cup freshly squeezed lime juice
   2 tbsp brown sugar
   2 tbsp dry mustard
   1 tsp dried leaf thyme
   1 tsp hot pepper sauce
   1/2 tsp salt
   1/2 tsp allspice
   Whirl, scraping down sides occasionally, until puréed.
Place
   6 skinless, boneless chicken breasts
   in a single layer in a dish. Spoon half of pepper mixture over top. Turn chicken. Smear on remaining mixture. Cover and refrigerate for 1 hour, preferably overnight.
Oil grill and preheat barbecue. Grill chicken, uncovered, until golden and springy to the touch, about 10 minutes per side. Serve with Sweet 'n' Sour Cucumber Salsa for a cooling effect (see recipe page 110).
Makes: 6 servings

PREPARATION: 20 MINUTES
MARINATE: 1 HOUR
GRILL: 20 MINUTES

MAPLE-SESAME CHICKEN WINGS

Make up a batch of these nibblers to serve with a bowl of sour cream.

In a large bowl, whisk together
   1/4 cup soy sauce
   1/4 cup pure maple syrup
   2 tbsp dark sesame oil
   2 tsp vegetable oil
   2 tbsp finely grated ginger
   3 crushed garlic cloves
Cut off and discard tips from
   4 lbs (2 kg) chicken wings
   Cut wings in half, through the joint. Then immerse wings in marinade. Stir well. Cover and refrigerate for at least 1 hour, preferably overnight.
Oil grill and preheat barbecue. Remove wings from marinade and place on grill. Barbecue with lid closed, turning often, until wings are well browned and no longer pink, about 30 minutes.
When done, place in a bowl and sprinkle with
   2 tbsp sesame seeds
   Toss and serve.
Makes: 4 servings

PREPARATION: 10 MINUTES
MARINATE: 1 HOUR
GRILL: 30 MINUTES

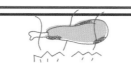

WARM HONEY CHICKEN SALAD

When you want a special lunch or light supper that's a departure from regular barbecue fare, present this salad supper.

In a small bowl, whisk together
   2 tbsp grainy mustard
   1 tbsp white or red wine vinegar
   1 tbsp liquid honey
   generous pinches of salt and pepper
While whisking continuously, drizzle in
   ¼ cup olive or vegetable oil
   (For a thinner dressing, whisk in 1 tbsp water.)
Set aside. If making ahead, leave dressing at room
   temperature for several hours or refrigerate.
Break into bite-size pieces
   1 small head red leaf lettuce
   1 small head radicchio
   1 Belgian endive (optional)
Arrange on 6 individual plates.

Oil grill and preheat barbecue. Place on grill
   6 skinless, boneless chicken breasts
   Barbecue, turning at least once, until chicken
   feels springy, about 12 to 15 minutes.
Transfer to a cutting board. Slice each breast
   crosswise into 5 or 6 slices. Arrange 1 breast
   on each salad plate. Drizzle with mustard
   dressing and serve.
Makes: 6 servings

PREPARATION: 15 MINUTES
GRILL: 15 MINUTES

WARM HONEY CHICKEN SALAD

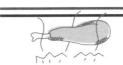

CHICKEN

GRILLED CITRUS THIGHS

Boneless chicken thighs are a great buy and as low-cal and nutritious as most other chicken parts.

Place

  8 chicken thighs, preferably boneless skin-side down, on cutting board. If not boneless, with a sharp knife, cut meat away from the bone. Remove skin, then flatten chicken slightly with your hand. Trim away any fat.

Stir together

  1/2 cup freshly squeezed lemon juice
  1/2 cup orange juice
  2 tbsp olive oil
  1/2 cup chopped fresh basil
    or 1 tbsp dried basil
  1/4 cup chopped fresh oregano
    or 1 tsp dried leaf oregano
  2 crushed garlic cloves
  3/4 tsp salt
  1/2 tsp ground black pepper

Place thighs in a shallow dish just large enough to snugly hold them or in a large self-sealing bag. Add about 3/4 of marinade and cover dish or seal bag. Marinate in refrigerator, turning once, at least 1 hour or overnight.

Oil grill and preheat barbecue. Drain marinade and discard. Grill thighs, brushing often with saved marinade, until golden, about 8 to 10 minutes per side. Serve with grilled potato slices and coleslaw.

Makes: 4 servings

PREPARATION: 20 MINUTES
MARINATE: 1 HOUR
GRILL: 16 MINUTES

BBQ ASIAN CHICKEN

This low-cal chicken gets an Oriental twist from a combination of everyday ingredients.

In a food processor, whirl until finely chopped

  2 whole green onions, cut into
    1-inch (2.5-cm) pieces
  2 whole garlic cloves, peeled
  2 tbsp dark sesame oil
  2 tbsp soy sauce
  2 tsp brown sugar
  1-inch (2.5-cm) piece fresh
    peeled ginger

Preheat barbecue. Place

  6 chicken thighs or 4 small chicken breasts
    or legs, about 1 lb (500 g)

on 6 pieces of foil large enough to wrap up and seal securely. Brush chicken with oil mixture. Save remaining sauce. Seal foil and place packets on grill. Heat for 15 minutes. Turn packets and continue heating for another 15 minutes.

Remove chicken from foil and discard juices. Place chicken directly on greased grill. Brush with remaining mixture. Grill for 10 minutes per side, turning often and brushing with sauce until chicken feels springy.

Makes: 4 servings

PREPARATION: 10 MINUTES
GRILL: 50 MINUTES

INDOOR SIZZLE:
For oven roasting, see page 42.

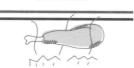

MAPLE CHICKEN & GRILLED FRUIT

*The winning combination of naturally sweet maple syrup and orange juice
flavors this finger-licking meal that can be cooked entirely on the grill.*

Oil grill and preheat barbecue. Stir together
- 1/2 cup frozen orange juice concentrate
- 1/2 cup maple syrup
- 1 tbsp vegetable or olive oil
- 1 tsp curry or ground cumin
- 1/4 tsp cayenne (optional)

Brush sauce over
- 8 skinless, boneless chicken breasts
- 3 sweet peppers, seeded and halved

Place on grill. Barbecue until underside of
chicken is golden, about 6 to 8 minutes. Turn
chicken and peppers, then brush with sauce.

Add to grill and brush with sauce
- 3 medium zucchini, sliced in half
- 2 oranges, cut into 1/2-inch (1-cm)
  thick slices (optional)
- 1 pineapple, peeled and sliced into
  1/2-inch (1-cm) slices

Continue cooking until chicken is golden, fruit
and zucchini are hot and peppers are tender,
about 6 to 10 more minutes. Turn zucchini
and fruit at least once.

Makes: 6 servings

> *PREPARATION: 15 MINUTES*
> *GRILL: 18 MINUTES*

MAPLE CHICKEN & GRILLED FRUIT

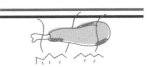

CHICKEN

FAST ROQUEFORT-LEMON CHICKEN

Instead of marinating, brush chicken with dressed-up bottled salad dressing for a speedy dinner.

Oil grill and preheat barbecue. Stir together
  ⅓ cup Roquefort dressing
    or other creamy blue cheese
    salad dressing
  1 tbsp freshly squeezed lemon juice
  2 crushed garlic cloves
  ½ tsp dried basil
  ½ tsp freshly ground black pepper
Brush over both sides of
  4 skinless, boneless chicken breasts
Grill chicken, brushing often with sauce, until
  golden and springy to the touch, about 8
  minutes per side.
  Makes: 4 servings

> *PREPARATION: 10 MINUTES*
> *GRILL: 16 MINUTES*

HONEY-GARLIC SANDWICHES

Topped with juicy mangoes and an Oriental honey baste, these sandwiches are extraordinary.

Oil grill and preheat barbecue. Lay
  4 skinless, boneless chicken breasts
  on a piece of waxed paper. With the bottom of
  your fist, gently pound, flattening slightly.
In a small bowl, stir together
  ¼ cup frozen orange juice concentrate
  2 tbsp soy sauce
  2 tbsp honey
  1 tsp lemon pepper
  1 large crushed garlic clove
Generously baste over chicken. Place on grill and
  barbecue until glazed, golden and springy to
  the touch, about 8 minutes per side. Turn
  often and brush with sauce.
Meanwhile, slice
  4 multigrain rolls or crusty buns
    or pita
  and line with several pieces of
  arugula or radicchio (optional)
Remove chicken to a cutting board and slice each
  breast, diagonally, into 3 or 4 pieces. Tuck into
  arugula-lined rolls.
  Makes: 4 servings

> *PREPARATION: 10 MINUTES*
> *GRILL: 16 MINUTES*

Fast Roquefort-Lemon Chicken

TIPS

Perfect Barbecued Chicken

Burning chicken on the barbecue seems to be a nationwide problem. The intense barbecue heat sears the chicken, but it takes a long time for the heat to cook through to the bones. To prevent burnt birds, microwave the chicken until amost cooked. Arrange chicken pieces in a single layer with thinner portions in centre of dish. Cover loosely with waxed paper. Microwave on high for 6 minutes per pound, rearranging chicken halfway through. Or prebake chicken pieces at 375°F (190°C) for 40 minutes. Then baste with barbecue sauce and grill on hot barbecue for 10 minutes.

Sizzling Wing Dips

Add zing to your wings with these dips:

- mash blue cheese into sour cream
- stir honey and fresh or ground ginger into yogurt
- mix equal amounts of mayonnaise and yogurt or sour cream and stir in your favorite spices, such as basil, oregano or thyme
- add hot pepper sauce or Worcestershire to your favorite bottled barbecue sauce
- stir sour cream and salsa together

BBQ Chicken Basics

- Tender foods such as chicken should be cooked over low heat. Either move grill several inches from coals or place on cooler area of grill. And always keep the lid closed or cover with a tent of aluminum foil.

- Marinades add extra flavor and moistness and tenderize chicken. But they often call for large quantities of fat. If you marinate chicken breasts in white wine or apple juice mixed with herbs for at least 4 hours or overnight, the liquid will be absorbed and the chicken will be wonderfully moist without the addition of any oil.

- To prevent sticking, instead of oiling the grill before heating, coat with a nonstick cooking spray.

- Instead of basting frantically with oil throughout barbecuing, just lightly brush the outside of chicken with oil before placing it on the grill.

- Always oil the grill before you turn on the barbecue. If you brush a hot grill, it can melt the brush, and if oil drips on coals, it may flare.

- Don't overcook small items. Boneless chicken needs only 8 to 10 minutes per side on a hot grill. It is done when chicken feels firm. For juicy bone-in chicken breasts and drumsticks, precook in microwave or wrap in foil and cook on barbecue until almost done. Lightly baste with barbecue sauce, garlic butter or a drizzle of oil and herbs. Then grill, turning often, until golden.

FISH & SEAFOOD

One bite and you'll be hooked on these succulent
GRILLED CARIBBEAN FISH STEAKS (see recipe page 58).
Treat with a silky coconut-citrus marinade
and they're ready in a mere 20 minutes.

FISH & SEAFOOD

TERIYAKI SALMON STEAKS

This Oriental sauce was designed for salmon and fast grilling. Serve with rice.

Oil grill and preheat barbecue. Stir together

2 tbsp sesame oil, preferably dark

2 tbsp soy sauce

1 tbsp brown sugar

1 tsp grated fresh ginger
    or bottled minced ginger

1 crushed garlic clove
    or ½ tsp bottled minced garlic

Generously brush sauce over

4 salmon steaks, at least
    1 inch (2.5 cm) thick

Barbecue salmon for 5 minutes, basting occasionally with teriyaki mixture. Turn and barbecue 4 or 5 more minutes, basting occasionally, until salmon flakes easily with a fork.
Makes: 4 servings

PREPARATION: 5 MINUTES
GRILL: 10 MINUTES

INDOOR SIZZLE:
For oven broiling, see below.

GRILLED BASIL SALMON

Salmon takes beautifully to a freshly made Dijon sauce. Garnish with fresh basil, coriander or chives.

Oil grill and preheat barbecue. In a small bowl, whisk together

¼ cup olive or vegetable oil

2 tbsp freshly squeezed lemon juice

1 tbsp Dijon mustard

2 tbsp finely chopped fresh basil
    or 1 tsp dried basil

¼ tsp freshly ground black pepper

pinch of salt

Brush sauce over

4 salmon steaks, at least 1 inch (2.5 cm) thick

Then place on grill and barbecue 4 to 5 minutes per side, brushing often with basil-oil mixture. Remove salmon to a platter and pour any remaining mixture over top.
Makes: 4 servings

PREPARATION: 5 MINUTES
GRILL: 10 MINUTES

INDOOR SIZZLE:
For oven broiling, see below.

INDOOR BROILING FOR YEAR-ROUND SIZZLE

Where a recipe indicates Indoor Sizzle, prepare fish as directed, but when it's time to barbecue, use this oven method instead. Preheat broiler. Place oven rack about 4 inches (10 cm) from broiler. Brush fish with mixture or marinade and place on a broiler pan. Broil for 4 to 5 minutes per side, brushing often with mixture, until fish flakes easily with a fork.

GRILLED SALMON STEAKS

This recipe is simplicity itself, but the combination of flavors can't be beat.

Oil grill and preheat barbecue. Whisk together
  3 tbsp vegetable oil
  2 tbsp freshly squeezed lemon juice
  ½ tsp freshly ground black pepper
Place on grill
  4 salmon steaks, at least 1 inch (2.5 cm) thick
Brush with oil mixture. Barbecue for 8 to
10 minutes, brushing with oil mixture and
carefully turning salmon after 5 minutes.
Makes: 4 servings

> PREPARATION: 5 MINUTES
> GRILL: 10 MINUTES

INDOOR SIZZLE:
For oven broiling, see page 56.

HONEY 'N' LIME GLAZED SALMON

A slightly sweet citrus glaze gives island taste to these gorgeous steaks.

Stir together
  finely grated peel of 1 lime
  juice of 2 limes, about ⅓ cup
  1 ½ tbsp Dijon mustard
  2 tbsp honey and ¼ tsp salt
Oil grill and preheat barbecue. Brush sauce over
  4 salmon steaks, at least 1 inch (2.5 cm) thick
Grill, basting often, until a knife tip inserted in the
  centre feels warm, about 5 minutes per side.
Makes: 4 servings

> PREPARATION: 5 MINUTES
> GRILL: 10 MINUTES

INDOOR SIZZLE:
For oven broiling, see page 56.

HONEY 'N' LIME GLAZED SALMON

FISH & SEAFOOD

GRILLED CARIBBEAN FISH STEAKS

For a stunning island taste, stir this lime-coconut milk baste together. Delicious on all meaty fish.

In a large shallow glass dish, stir together
- 14-oz (400-mL) can unsweetened coconut milk
- ¼ cup freshly squeezed lime juice
- ¼ cup finely chopped hot peppers
- 4 large crushed garlic cloves
- 2 tsp paprika
- 1 tsp turmeric
- ¼ tsp salt

Add
- 6 to 8 fish steaks, such as grouper, tuna, swordfish or sea bass fillets, at least 1 inch (2.5 cm) thick

and turn once or twice so they are well coated. Cover and refrigerate for at least 1 hour, preferably overnight. Turn partway through.

Lightly oil grill and preheat barbecue. Place fish on grill and barbecue for about 5 minutes per side or until a knife point inserted into the centre feels warm. At the same time, simmer marinade in a small pan on the stove for at least 5 minutes. Then pour over grilled steaks.

Makes: 6 to 8 servings

PREPARATION: 10 MINUTES
MARINATE: 1 HOUR
GRILL: 10 MINUTES

INDOOR SIZZLE:
For oven broiling, see page 56.

CURRIED HALIBUT STEAKS

Sweet, mild, moist — fresh halibut is always a treat.

Whisk together
- 3 tbsp freshly squeezed lemon juice
- 2 tbsp olive or vegetable oil
- 1 tbsp finely chopped coriander or parsley
- 1 tsp curry powder
- ½ tsp ground cumin
- generous pinches of salt and cayenne pepper

On a large plate, place
- 4 thick halibut steaks, at least 1 inch (2.5 cm) thick

Spoon half of marinade over fish. Turn and spoon remaining marinade over top. Cover and marinate at room temperature for 30 minutes.

Oil grill and preheat barbecue. Grill halibut for about 5 to 7 minutes per side, until a knife point inserted in the centre feels warm.

Makes: 4 servings

PREPARATION: 10 MINUTES
MARINATE: 30 MINUTES
GRILL: 14 MINUTES

INDOOR SIZZLE:
For oven broiling, see page 56.

TERIYAKI HALIBUT STEAKS

Gracefully glaze halibut steaks with this citrus-soy baste. It's perfection itself.

Oil grill and preheat barbecue. Stir together
  2 tbsp olive or vegetable oil
  2 tbsp frozen orange juice concentrate
  2 tbsp soy sauce
  generous pinches of ground ginger
Brush over
  4 halibut steaks, at least 1 inch (2.5 cm) thick
Place on grill and barbecue, covered, for about 10 to 15 minutes, turning several times and brushing with marinade.
Makes: 4 servings

PREPARATION: 10 MINUTES
GRILL: 15 MINUTES

INDOOR SIZZLE:
For oven broiling, see page 56.

PACIFIC RIM SNAPPER

Here's a quick way to grill whole snapper without fish falling through the grate.

Oil grill and preheat barbecue. Fill cavity of
  2 whole red snappers
  with
  fresh coriander leaves
  thin slices of 1 lime
Generously brush both sides of fish with
  hoisin sauce
Place each on a large piece of lightly oiled heavy aluminum foil. Seal foil and place on hot grill. Barbecue for about 15 minutes per side for 1½-inch (4-cm) thick fish.
Makes: 4 servings

PREPARATION: 10 MINUTES
GRILL: 30 MINUTES

PACIFIC RIM SNAPPER

FISH & SEAFOOD

OUTSTANDING ORANGE ROUGHY

Follow our easy foil-wrap method and dress up low-cal tender fillets with a sophisticated broth.

Preheat barbecue. Lay on 4 pieces of
   heavy-duty foil
   1½ lbs (750 g) orange roughy fillets,
      cut into 4 serving-size pieces
Pour over each
   1 tbsp white wine
   Sprinkle generously with
   salt
   freshly ground white or black pepper
   Lay on top
   sprigs of fresh dill
   2 lemon or lime slices
Bring long edges of foil together, fold over
   several times and seal ends.
Lay packets, seam-side up, on grill. Grill for 9 to
   10 minutes. Do not turn over or juices may
   leak out. Place packets on heated plates. Let
   guests open their own packets. Serve with
   grilled potatoes and vegetables.
Makes: 4 servings

PREPARATION: 5 MINUTES
GRILL: 10 MINUTES

NIÇOISE TUNA STEAKS

Tuna steaks are expensive, and this fashionably robust tomato-and-olive relish more than does them justice.

Oil grill and preheat barbecue. Whisk together
   ¼ cup vegetable oil
   2 tbsp freshly squeezed lemon juice
   2 tsp anchovy paste
   1 tsp Dijon mustard
To make a fresh tomato-olive relish,
   stir 2 tbsp of this mixture with
   2 ripe tomatoes, peeled and finely chopped
   ¼ cup black olives, finely chopped
   1 tsp dried basil
   ½ tsp granulated sugar
Generously brush remaining oil mixture over
   4 tuna steaks or other firm-fleshed
      fish steaks, at least 1 inch (2.5 cm) thick
Barbecue about 4 to 5 minutes per side,
   turning carefully and brushing often with oil
   mixture. Remove to a platter. Pour remaining
   oil mixture over top. Spoon fresh tomato-
   olive mixture over each steak.
Makes: 4 servings

PREPARATION: 12 MINUTES
GRILL: 10 MINUTES

INDOOR SIZZLE:
For oven broiling, see page 56.

FISH & CHIPS ON THE BARBIE

This recipe gives new meaning to fish and chips. Not only have we turned up the flavor, but we've eliminated the tasteless batter.

Partially bake
 4 unpeeled baking potatoes
 in a 400°F (200°C) oven for 30 minutes or in the microwave for 6 minutes. Then cut potatoes into 1-inch (2.5-cm) slices.

Oil grill and preheat barbecue. Stir together
 ¼ cup olive oil
 2 crushed garlic cloves
 ¼ tsp each paprika, salt and black pepper
 Generously brush oil on potatoes and place on grill, cut-side down. Grill, basting frequently and turning, until a golden brown, about 20 to 25 minutes.

Meanwhile, stir together
 ¼ cup melted butter
 2 tsp hot pepper sauce
Squeeze
 juice of 1 lemon
 over both sides of
 4 fish steaks, such as tuna or salmon
 Then brush with butter mixture.

Place on grill and barbecue, turning once and basting frequently, about 5 to 6 minutes per side.

Makes: 4 servings

> *PREPARATION: 15 MINUTES*
> *MICROWAVE: 6 MINUTES*
> *GRILL: 25 MINUTES*

FISH & CHIPS ON THE BARBIE

FISH & SEAFOOD

GRILLED WHOLE HADDOCK

Grilling a whole fish is a fast and flavorful way to speed up dinner.

Sprinkle
    freshly ground white pepper
into the cavity of
    3-lb (1.5-kg) whole haddock
    Fill with
    sprigs of fresh dill or dried dillweed
    thin slices of lemon or lime
    Brush outside of haddock with
    vegetable or sesame oil

Measure thickness of fish at thickest part. A 3-lb (1.5-kg) whole haddock will be about 2 inches (5 cm) thick. Allow 10 minutes grilling time for each inch of thickness.

Place fish in a greased fish basket and add a few sprigs of dill if you wish. Close basket and place on grill. If you do not have a basket, place fish on a greased grill. Keep barbecue lid closed. Barbecue for 10 minutes per side, carefully turning partway through grilling.

Makes: 4 servings

PREPARATION: 5 MINUTES
GRILL: 20 MINUTES

ORIENTAL SHRIMP SATAY

Here's a fast route to a superb satay appetizer. Serve with peanut sauce for dipping.

Stir together
    1/3 cup light soy sauce
    1 tbsp brown sugar
    1 tbsp sherry
    1 tbsp lime juice
    1 tbsp grated fresh ginger
    1 crushed garlic clove

Thread onto skewers
    24 large shelled shrimp
and place in a shallow glass dish just large enough to hold them. Pour marinade over top, cover and refrigerate for at least 30 minutes, but no more than 1 hour.

Drain skewers and discard marinade. Grill on a preheated barbecue for about 3 to 4 minutes per side. Serve with bottled or freshly made Peanut Sauce (see recipe page 114), plum sauce or tahini for dipping. For an easy main course, serve with rice pilaf and stir-fried broccoli and red peppers.

Makes: 8 skewers

PREPARATION: 10 MINUTES
MARINATE: 30 MINUTES
GRILL: 8 MINUTES

VARIATION: Instead of shrimp, use
    1 lb (500 g) skinless, boneless chicken breasts. Cut into 1/4-inch (0.5-cm) slices, then into 3-inch (8-cm) pieces. Thread onto skewers and proceed as above.

HOT GRILLED SOUTHERN SHRIMP

*An orange juice baste spiked with a sprinkle of cayenne provides some spice to tender shrimp.
Finish with a sophisticated sauce of roasted sweet peppers.*

Lightly oil grill and preheat barbecue. Thread
   onto skewers
   2 lbs (1 kg) large raw shrimp (see note)
   To keep the curled shape, thread each shrimp
   twice, once through the thick end, then near
   the tail.
Stir together
   ¼ cup frozen orange juice concentrate
   2 tbsp olive oil
   2 crushed garlic cloves
   ½ tsp salt
   ¼ tsp cayenne pepper
Brush over shrimp. Place on barbecue and grill,
   brushing often with orange mixture, until

shrimp are bright pink and hot, about 3 to
4 minutes per side. Sprinkle with
2 tbsp chopped parsley or
   fresh coriander (optional)
Serve with Roasted Red Pepper Sauce (see recipe
   page 110) for dipping.
Makes: 6 servings

PREPARATION: 10 MINUTES
GRILL: 8 MINUTES

NOTE: *For juicy shrimp, grill with the shell on.
   If you remove shell before grilling, leave tail
   attached to use as a handle when eating.*

HOT GRILLED SOUTHERN SHRIMP

FISH & SEAFOOD

CHILI SHRIMPS

*When you're pressed for time, but want to create
a knockout dinner, this is the number.*

In a large bowl, combine
  6-oz (175-mL) container
    or ¾ cup plain yogurt
  3 tbsp chili sauce or salsa
  1 tbsp olive or vegetable oil
Stir any or all of the following additions into
yogurt mixture:
  2 tbsp finely chopped fresh coriander
  2 tsp finely grated fresh ginger
  ¼ to ½ tsp cayenne pepper
Peel and devein
  1 lb (500 g) medium-size or large shrimps
If using frozen shrimps, rinse under cold
  running water to remove ice crystals. Then
  thaw and pat dry. Add shrimps to yogurt
  mixture. Stir until evenly coated and cover.
  Refrigerate for 30 minutes.
Oil grill and preheat barbecue. Thread coated
  shrimps onto skewers. Place kebabs on
  greased grill and barbecue for about 3 to
  4 minutes per side, depending on size of
  shrimps, turning occasionally, until shrimps
  are bright pink.
Makes: 3 to 4 servings

PREPARATION: 15 MINUTES
MARINATE: 30 MINUTES
GRILL: 8 MINUTES

MUSSELS ON THE GRILL

*Yes, mussels can be cooked on the barbecue.
Serve as an appetizer for four or dinner for two.*

Preheat barbecue. Scrub under cold running
  water and remove any beards from
  3 lbs (1.5 kg) fresh mussels
Discard any mussels that are open and will
  not close when gently tapped. Drain well.
  Place in a large foil lasagna pan or other large,
  shallow metal pan that will fit on the
  barbecue, such as a 9x13-inch (3-L) pan.
Stir together
  ¼ cup dry white wine
  ½ tbsp olive oil
  3 crushed garlic cloves
  Pour over mussels.
Sprinkle with
  4 firm tomatoes, seeded and chopped
  4 green onions, thinly sliced
  1 tsp hot red pepper flakes or 2 jalapeño
    peppers, seeded and finely chopped
Tightly seal pan using foil. Grill right away or
  refrigerate up to 6 hours.
Place sealed foil pan on barbecue. Cook until
  foil pan is hot and domed. Mussels should be
  open and broth hot, about 15 minutes, or
  18 minutes if pan has been refrigerated.
  Discard any mussels that have not opened.
  Serve right away from foil pan or in heated
  serving bowls. Dip crusty bread into broth.
Makes: 2 main courses or appetizers for 4

PREPARATION: 15 MINUTES
GRILL: 15 MINUTES

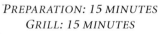

Mussels on the Grill

BARBECUED STEAMED CLAMS

*Cook clams or mussels right on the barbie
for an easy appetizer.*

Scrub under cold running water
 3 lbs (1.5 kg) clams or mussels
 Place clams in a sink full of salted cold water.
 Swish clams in water to remove sand. Then
 drain water and repeat cleaning several times.
 Mussels only need scrubbing and any beards
 removed.

Wrap clams or mussels in foil and grill for about
 8 to 10 minutes or just until shells open. Or
 place right on the grill until they pop wide
 open, about 5 to 7 minutes. Use toothpicks or
 small skewers to remove the clams. Enjoy as is
 or dip in a hot pepper sauce or salsa.
 Makes: 4 servings

PREPARATION: 5 MINUTES
GRILL: 10 MINUTES

TERIYAKI SCALLOP KEBABS

*Sherry and fresh ginger make a luxurious coating
for sweet scallops — perfect for a special party.*

In a small bowl, stir together
 ¼ cup soy sauce
 1 tsp sherry
 1 tsp freshly grated ginger
  or ¼ tsp ground ginger
 ½ tsp brown sugar
Rinse under cold water
 1 lb (500 g) large sea scallops
 Drain well. Remove the opaque tough muscle
 on the side of the scallop, because it remains
 tough, even after cooking. Place scallops in
 sauce and stir to coat.

Thread scallops onto skewers alternating with
 1 green pepper, cut into
  1-inch (2.5-cm) pieces
 5 to 10 cherry tomatoes
Oil grill and preheat barbecue. Barbecue kebabs,
 basting often with soy marinade, turning at
 least once, for about 8 minutes.
 Makes: 3 to 4 servings

PREPARATION: 20 MINUTES
GRILL: 8 MINUTES

MEDITERRANEAN SEAFOOD SKEWERS

*Give succulent shrimp kebabs a Mediterranean
touch with a herb-olive oil baste.*

Oil grill and preheat barbecue.
 In a small bowl, stir together
 ¼ cup olive oil
 1 tsp dried basil
 ¼ tsp leaf oregano
 ¼ tsp lemon pepper
Thread skewers with pieces of
 ½ small lemon, cut into ¼-inch
  (0.5-cm) slices and halved
 alternating with
 1 lb (500 g) large shrimps,
  peeled and deveined
 12 to 15 pimento-stuffed olives
  or slices of thin zucchini
 2 sweet peppers, cut into
  1-inch (2.5-cm) pieces
Brush kebabs with oil mixture. Barbecue for
 about 3 minutes per side, depending on size
 of shrimps, turning occasionally, until
 shrimps are bright pink.
 Makes: 3 to 4 servings

PREPARATION: 15 MINUTES
GRILL: 6 MINUTES

FISH & SEAFOOD

SENSATIONAL GRILLED LOBSTER

Lobster is always a treat. Cooking it on the barbie adds that little extra something.

Prepare
> Shallot-Wine Butter Sauce (see recipe this page or use garlic butter, homemade or store-bought)

To slightly precook lobster, bring a large pot of water to a boil. Add
> 4 live lobsters, each about 1 ½ lbs (750 g)

Boil for 5 minutes. Drain.

Oil grill and preheat barbecue. Place the lobster on the grill with the rounded top-side down and belly-side up. Cover and grill for 20 minutes, turning every 5 minutes. Serve immediately with warm Shallot-Wine Butter Sauce or garlic butter. A tossed green salad and crusty bread complete the feast.
Makes: 4 servings

> *PREPARATION: 15 MINUTES*
> *COOK: 5 MINUTES*
> *GRILL: 20 MINUTES*

LOBSTER BARBECUE FEAST

Simply heat precooked lobsters on the barbecue and baste with butter sauce for a truly decadent taste.

Prepare double portion
> Shallot-Wine Butter Sauce (see recipe this page)

Using a very sharp knife, slice in half lengthwise down the back and through the tail of
> 8 cooked lobsters, each about 1 ½ lbs (750 g)

Lightly crack claws.
Remove gills and greyish sack near head.

Oil grill and preheat barbecue. Place lobster, shell-side down, on grill. Generously brush flesh with butter sauce. Cover and grill for 5 minutes if lobsters were at room temperature or 10 minutes if lobsters were chilled. Brush often with butter sauce. Then turn flesh-side down and grill just until flesh starts to take on a golden edge, about 3 minutes. Serve with warm butter sauce for dipping.
Makes: 8 servings

> *PREPARATION: 15 MINUTES*
> *GRILL: 13 MINUTES*

SHALLOT-WINE BUTTER SAUCE

This sauce is fabulous with lobster or shrimp for basting or dipping. Or drizzle over any fish.

In a small saucepan or frying pan, combine
> 1 cup dry white wine
> ½ cup finely chopped shallots
> 1 tsp chopped jalapeño peppers (optional)
> ¼ tsp salt

Boil, uncovered, over medium-high heat, until wine is reduced to about ½ cup, about 10 to 12 minutes. Reduce heat to medium.

Cut into 8 to 10 pieces
> ⅓ cup cold unsalted butter

Add butter piece by piece to simmering mixture, whisking each time until butter is melted, about 6 minutes. Sauce will thicken. Taste and add more salt if needed. Serve right away or cover and refrigerate up to a week.
Makes: ¾ cup, enough for 4 lobsters

> *PREPARATION: 15 MINUTES*
> *COOK: 18 MINUTES*

GRILLED CALAMARI

*A seafood of great versatility, squid or calamari (its Italian name)
is now widely available cleaned and ready for grilling.*

Oil grill and preheat barbecue. Stir together
  ¼ cup soy sauce
  1 tbsp sesame oil
  2 tsp chili-garlic sauce or Sambal Oelek
    (a fiery chili sauce)
Place
  2 lbs (1 kg) calamari, cleaned
  in a large self-sealing bag.

Add the soy mixture and move calamari
around until evenly coated. Use right away
or refrigerate for 1 or 2 hours.
Place calamari on the grill and barbecue,
turning often, for 8 to 15 minutes depending
on the size.
Makes: 3 to 4 servings

PREPARATION: 5 MINUTES
GRILL: 15 MINUTES

TIPS

BBQ Fish Basics

- Good fish choices for the barbecue include
such firm-fleshed fish as salmon, tuna or
swordfish. They hold together well, even when
cooked, and are usually sold at least 1 inch
(2.5 cm) thick.

- Not recommended for the barbecue are such
delicate fish as sole, turbot and most trout.
They are not only soft in texture, but they come
in thin long fillets that don't hold together well
when turning.

- To turn delicate fish, place fish steaks in an
oiled fish barbecue basket, or loosely wrap
whole fish in oiled chicken wire. Cook over
low heat or on cooler areas of grill.

- Don't oil the skin when barbecuing fillets.
Place fillets skin-side down on the barbecue,
then when it's time to turn them, carefully work
a thin spatula between the skin and the flesh
and turn the fish leaving the skin on the grill.

- Foil wrapping is an easy way to turn a whole or
delicate-fleshed fish on the grill, but remember
that the fish is being steamed in its own juices,
rather than barbecued.

- Don't overcook small items. Fish steaks
that are 1 inch (2.5 cm) thick need about
10 minutes on a hot grill, turning partway
through. Shrimp or ½-inch (1-cm) fish
fillets need only 5 to 7 minutes, turning
partway through. Fish is done when a knife
inserted in the centre feels warm when
removed.

- Don't marinate fish or seafood very long.
Most fish is already tender, so marinating is
not needed as a tenderizer. Also, you don't
want the marinade to overpower the delicate
taste of the fish.

- If using frozen shrimp, rinse under cold water
to remove ice crystals. Then thaw and pat dry
before using.

FRUIT

*Grill these colorful HOT PINEAPPLE & BERRY KEBABS (see recipe page 70)
along with TENDER GARLIC LAMB KEBABS (see recipe page 82)
for an easy-going dinner. Or for dessert, serve on pretty plates with
a spoonful of sweetened sour cream topped with lime zest curls.*

FRUIT

Pineapple-Mango Sundae

Make the most of very ripe mangoes by simply puréeing them into this passion fruit sauce.

Oil grill and preheat barbecue. Peel
    1 pineapple
    and slice ¾ inch (2 cm) thick.
    Barbecue slices 4 minutes per side, until hot.
Meanwhile, peel
    1 mango
    then purée in a blender with
    1 tbsp lemon juice
Taste, and add sugar if necessary, or water if too thick. Top each grilled pineapple slice with
    a scoop of ice cream
    then drizzle with mango purée.
Makes: 4 servings

PREPARATION: 20 MINUTES
GRILL: 8 MINUTES

Hot Pineapple & Berry Kebabs

Grill these kebabs along with lamb for dinner. Or serve for dessert with sweetened sour cream.

In a large bowl, combine
    1 pineapple, peeled and sliced into pieces
    1 box strawberries, hulled
    juice of 1 lime
Just before barbecuing, add
    2 firm bananas,
        sliced into 1-inch (2.5-cm) pieces
Sprinkle with
    2 tbsp granulated sugar
    and stir gently until coated.
Oil grill and preheat barbecue. Thread fruit onto skewers, about 5 to 6 pieces per skewer. Place on grill and barbecue, turning often and basting with remaining juices, just until hot, about 6 to 10 minutes.
Makes: 4 servings

PREPARATION: 20 MINUTES
GRILL: 10 MINUTES

Grilled Mangoes

Choose ripe mangoes that are not yet soft and oil grill well to avoid slices careening through the grate.

Oil grill and preheat barbecue. Stir together
    2 tbsp melted butter
    2 tbsp liquid honey
    ¼ tsp ground ginger
With a sharp knife or large vegetable peeler, slice peel from
    2 firm but ripe large mangoes
Then slice mango in large pieces. Brush with honey mixture and place on grill. Barbecue, basting often with honey mixture, until mango is hot and golden grill marks appear, about 2 to 3 minutes per side. Serve warm with grilled chicken or around coffee or French vanilla ice cream.
Makes: 4 servings

PREPARATION: 10 MINUTES
GRILL: 6 MINUTES

Grilled Pineapple

Lend a tropical accent to any alfresco meal with this simply grilled pineapple.

Oil grill and preheat barbecue. Slice peel from
    1 ripe pineapple
    Quarter pineapple lengthwise.
    Lightly brush with
    2 tbsp melted butter or vegetable oil
Barbecue, turning pineapple frequently and brushing occasionally with butter or oil, until heated through, about 10 minutes. Wonderful with grilled pork tenderloin or spicy chicken. For dessert, serve with coconut ice cream.
Makes: 4 servings

PREPARATION: 5 MINUTES
GRILL: 10 MINUTES

WARM FRUIT DESSERT PIZZA

This is one of the easiest glamour desserts you can make for a dinner party.
Also great as appetizers. And kids love it!

Oil grill and preheat barbecue. Place
　1 store-bought pizza crust
top-side down, on grill. Barbecue just until golden, about 2 minutes. Turn crust over and barbecue until golden, about 2 to 5 more minutes.

Remove from grill and immediately spread with
　¾ cup spreadable cream cheese or
　　creamy chèvre
Then arrange on cheese
　3 cups sliced fruit, such as plums,
　　strawberries and nectarines

Slice pizza into wedges and serve warm.
　Makes: 8 servings

PREPARATION: 15 MINUTES
GRILL: 7 MINUTES

INDOOR SIZZLE: *Oven Baking*
Preheat oven to 425°F (220°C).
Place store-bought pizza crust right on oven rack with top-side up. For even browning, do not place on a pan. Then bake until evenly golden, about 8 to 10 minutes, checking after 5 minutes. Continue following recipe above.

WARM FRUIT DESSERT PIZZA

FRUIT

TROPICAL FRUIT KEBABS

These glamorous cinnamon-scented kebabs need only a bowl of tangy yogurt for dipping.

Oil grill and preheat barbecue. In a small bowl, stir together
  1/4 cup melted butter
  3 tbsp brown sugar
  1 tbsp freshly squeezed lemon juice
  1/4 tsp ground cinnamon
Thread skewers with
  1 firm ripe nectarine or peach,
    cut into bite-size wedges
  alternating with pieces of
  1 large firm ripe banana,
    peeled and cut into 2-inch (5-cm) chunks
  1 cup strawberries, hulled
  1 kiwi, peeled and
    cut into 1/2-inch (1-cm) wedges
  1/2 (10-oz/298-g) pkg store-bought
    frozen pound cake, cut into 1 1/2-inch
    (4-cm) cubes (optional)
Brush kebabs with spiced-butter mixture. Barbecue for 5 to 8 minutes or until cake and fruit are warm and slightly glazed. Turn often and brush with butter mixture. Yogurt makes a wonderful healthy dipping sauce.
Makes: 6 servings

PREPARATION: 10 MINUTES
GRILL: 8 MINUTES

GRILLED GLAZED NECTARINES

Nectarines or peaches are a cooling accompaniment for spicy grilled chicken.

Oil grill and preheat barbecue. Then wash
  4 nectarines or peaches, preferably freestone
  If using peaches, plunge into rapid boiling water for 30 to 60 seconds to loosen skins. Rinse under cold running water, then peel. Slice nectarines into halves or quarters, depending on size. Do not peel nectarines.
Stir together
  2 tbsp brown sugar
  2 tbsp melted butter
  1 tbsp orange or almond liqueur
    or rum (optional)
  pinch of cayenne pepper (optional)
Brush over fruit and grill, basting often, until hot and golden grill marks appear, about 2 to 3 minutes per side. Serve warm. Also good with frozen yogurt or ice cream and a drizzle of Amaretto.
Makes: 3 to 4 servings

PREPARATION: 10 TO 15 MINUTES
GRILL: 6 MINUTES

Tropical Fruit Kebabs

FAST BBQ PEACH PACKAGES

A peach warmed in butter-rum sauce, served with French vanilla ice cream, makes a glamorous finale.

Place
   1 sliced peach
   on a 12-inch (30-cm) square of foil. Dot with
   ½ tsp butter
Sprinkle with
   ½ tsp brown sugar
   2 tbsp rum or orange liqueur (optional)
Seal foil tightly and barbecue 8 minutes per side.
   Serve with grilled chicken as an entrée or
   around butter pecan ice cream or frozen
   yogurt for dessert.
   Makes: 2 servings

PREPARATION: 5 MINUTES
GRILL: 16 MINUTES

HONEY GRILLED PEARS

It's hard to find a sexier appetizer than warm pears surrounded with a crumbling of blue cheese.

Slice in half, then core
   ripe pears
   Baste with
   maple syrup or apple juice,
      sweetened with a little honey
Place pears on a greased grill and cook, basting
   and turning often, until pears take on a
   golden hue, from 5 to 8 minutes. Remove to a
   plate and crumble over top
   a little blue cheese or chèvre
Serve warm on salad greens or with grilled
   chicken, pork or lamb.

PREPARATION: 5 MINUTES
GRILL: 8 MINUTES

FRUIT

TIPS

BBQ Fruit Basics

- Good fruit choices for grilling are firm bananas, fresh pineapple, pears, apples, thick slices of mango, peaches and nectarines.

- Poor fruit choices are any fruit that has a high water content such as watermelon, oranges and soft fruits such as kiwi.

- To prevent fruit from sticking to the grill, brush with maple syrup, orange juice concentrate, nut-flavored liqueurs, rum or sherry. This will speed up the browning and quickly create a caramelized area on the fruit's surface before it becomes hot and turns mushy.

- Add a little butter to a fruit base. It adds a lot more taste than oil and helps the fruit from drying out.

- Boost the flavor after grilling by squeezing a little lime or lemon juice over the fruit as soon as it's removed from the grill. If serving with meat, a spritz of balsamic vinegar is good.

- If basting with orange or apple juices, add pinches of cinnamon, nutmeg or allspice for bananas, apples or pears; or cumin or curry if serving the fruit with chicken or meat.

Fruit and Meat Combos

- Apples and pears go well with barbecued pork chops, ribs or chicken.

- Mango is good with chicken and some fish.

- Pineapple is superb with pork or chicken.

- Peaches or nectarines go well with chicken, ribs, lamb or chicken.

KEBABS

*Amazingly enough, the baste for these SOUTHWESTERN KEBABS
(see recipe page 80) is made with only two ingredients —
salsa and plum sauce — and takes only 10 minutes of preparation.
Serve on a bed of Italian rice. A real winner with kids.*

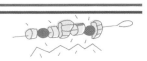

KEBABS

GINGER CHICKEN KEBABS

Ground coriander and lime juice add exotic undertones to these fast chicken kebabs.

Whisk together
    2 tbsp peanut or vegetable oil
    2 tbsp freshly squeezed lime juice
    1 tbsp soy sauce
    2 tsp freshly grated ginger
        or bottled minced ginger
    1 tsp ground coriander
    1/4 tsp salt
    1/4 tsp freshly ground black pepper
    generous pinch of hot red pepper flakes
Add to marinade and stir until coated
    4 skinless, boneless chicken breasts, sliced
        into 1 1/2-inch (4-cm) cubes
    Cover and refrigerate for at least 1 hour,
    preferably overnight, stirring occasionally.
Oil grill and preheat barbecue. Thread skewers
    with chicken alternating with pieces of
    1 sweet pepper, red or yellow,
        sliced into 1-inch (2.5-cm) pieces
    1 green zucchini,
        sliced into 1/2-inch (1-cm) rounds
Place kebabs on grill. Barbecue, turning
    occasionally, until chicken feels firm, about
    8 to 10 minutes. Serve over, or alongside, rice.
Makes: 4 servings

PREPARATION: 10 MINUTES
MARINATE: 1 HOUR
GRILL: 10 MINUTES

CUMIN-HONEY CHICKEN KEBABS

Use everyday ingredients to lace boneless chicken breasts with an intriguing sweet glaze.

Oil grill and preheat barbecue. Slice lengthwise
    4 skinless, boneless chicken breasts
        each into 3 long strips. Thread onto skewers.
Whisk together
    1/4 cup olive or vegetable oil
    1 tbsp soy sauce
    1 tsp liquid honey
    1 tsp ground cumin
    1/8 tsp cayenne
    Liberally brush over chicken strips.
Barbecue with lid closed or covered with a foil
    tent, basting often with sauce for the first 3
    minutes and turning several times until
    chicken feels springy, about 10 minutes.
Makes: 4 servings

PREPARATION: 10 MINUTES
GRILL: 10 MINUTES

INDOOR SIZZLE:
For oven broiling, see below.

INDOOR BROILING FOR YEAR-ROUND SIZZLE

Where a recipe indicates Indoor Sizzle, prepare meat or fish as directed, but when it's time to barbecue, use this oven method instead. For chicken, lamb or fish kebabs, set on a rack on a baking sheet 4 inches (10 cm) from preheated broiler. Broil, about 10 minutes, turning often and basting with marinade for the first 4 minutes of cooking. For sausage, pork or ham kebabs, set rack 6 inches (15 cm) from preheated broiler. Broil for 6 to 8 minutes per side, brushing with marinade and turning occasionally.

FAR EASTERN KEBABS

Sesame oil gives an intriguing Oriental taste to these glorious chicken kebabs.
Wonderful with grilled peppers and steamed rice.

Oil grill and preheat barbecue. Stir together
  2 tbsp soy sauce
  1 tbsp sesame oil
  1 tsp granulated sugar
  2 tbsp freshly grated ginger
  2 crushed garlic cloves
  ¼ tsp hot pepper sauce
Stir into marinade until well coated
  4 skinless, boneless chicken breasts,
    cut into 1-inch (2.5-cm) wide strips
  Thread onto skewers. Barbecue right away or
  refrigerate for an hour or two.

Generously brush kebabs with baste and barbecue with lid closed or covered with a foil tent, basting often with sauce for the first 3 minutes and turning several times until chicken feels springy, about 10 minutes.
Makes: 4 servings

PREPARATION: 15 MINUTES
GRILL: 10 MINUTES

INDOOR SIZZLE:
For oven broiling, see page 76.

FAR EASTERN KEBABS

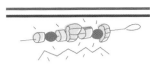

KEBABS

HOT MEATBALL KEBABS

Meatballs are sure winners at any party. With this version, you don't have to labor over a hot stove.

Oil grill and preheat barbecue. In a large bowl, whisk together
  1 egg
  2 tbsp chili sauce or ketchup
  1 tbsp horseradish
  1 tsp leaf thyme
  ½ tsp salt
  ½ tsp freshly ground black pepper
  pinch of cayenne pepper
Add
  1 lb (500 g) ground beef or veal
Stir in
  ⅓ cup fine dry bread crumbs
Work with a fork or your hands until blended. Form into meatballs, about 1½ inches (4 cm) wide. This will make about 20 meatballs. Carefully thread 3 or 4 meatballs, leaving ¼-inch (0.5-cm) space between each to ensure even cooking, onto each skewer. (Nine-inch skewers work best for this recipe.) Once meatballs are on skewers, gently squeeze to help them adhere.
Place kebabs on grill and barbecue with lid closed, for 10 minutes, turning often, for well-done.
Meanwhile, split in half lengthwise
  6-inch crusty submarine
    or kaiser rolls or tortillas
  During last minute of grilling, place rolls on barbecue to toast. Serve meatballs in rolls, topped with grated cheese, lettuce and chopped tomatoes.
Makes: 4 to 6 servings

PREPARATION: 15 MINUTES
GRILL: 10 MINUTES

HERBED CHICKEN KEBABS

When you want a light dinner for two — these lemon-scented kebabs are your answer.

In a medium-size bowl, stir together
  2 tbsp olive oil
  2 tbsp freshly squeezed lemon juice
  1 crushed garlic clove
  ½ tsp dried leaf thyme or basil
  generous pinches of salt, white pepper and granulated sugar
Stir in
  2 large skinless, boneless chicken breasts, sliced into 1½-inch (4-cm) pieces
Press a piece of clear wrap onto surface. Refrigerate for at least 30 minutes.
Oil grill and preheat barbecue. Remove chicken pieces from marinade and set marinade aside. Thread chicken pieces onto skewers, alternating with pieces of
  1 zucchini, sliced into
    ¼-inch (0.5-cm) rounds
  1 sweet pepper, seeded and cut into
    1-inch (2.5-cm) pieces
Generously brush kebabs with baste and barbecue with lid closed or covered with a foil tent. Turn several times until chicken feels springy, about 10 minutes.
Makes: 2 servings

PREPARATION: 10 MINUTES
MARINATE: 30 MINUTES
GRILL: 10 MINUTES

INDOOR SIZZLE:
For oven broiling, see page 76.

78

LIGHTLY CURRIED CHICKEN KEBABS

Serve these kebabs with basmati rice and yogurt, sour cream or peanut sauce for dipping.

Oil grill and preheat barbecue. In a small bowl, whisk together
>3 tbsp soy sauce
>2 tbsp peanut or vegetable oil
>1 tbsp brown sugar
>1 tbsp lime or lemon juice
>1 crushed garlic clove
>1 tsp curry powder
>½ tsp ground coriander
>½ tsp ground cumin

Thread
>4 skinless, boneless chicken breasts, sliced into 1-inch (2.5-cm) wide strips

onto skewers by weaving skewers in and out of chicken strips so chicken lies flat.

Generously brush kebabs with baste and barbecue with lid closed or covered with a foil tent, basting often with sauce and turning several times until chicken feels springy, about 10 minutes.

Makes: 4 servings

PREPARATION: 10 MINUTES
GRILL: 10 MINUTES

INDOOR SIZZLE:
For oven broiling, see page 76.

ORANGE PORK KEBABS

These lean kebabs are kept moist and flavorful with sage, Dijon, orange and honey.

Oil grill and preheat barbecue. In a small bowl, stir together
>⅓ cup vegetable oil
>1 tbsp Dijon mustard
>finely grated peel of ½ orange
>¾ tsp rubbed sage (not ground)
>½ tsp liquid honey (optional)
>2 crushed garlic cloves
>generous grinding of black pepper

Thread skewers with
>1 pork tenderloin, about ¾ lb (375 g), cut into 1-inch (2.5-cm) cubes

alternating with
>1 small sweet green pepper, seeded and cut into 1-inch (2.5-cm) pieces
>½ small orange, cut into ¼-inch (0.5-cm) slices and halved

Brush kebabs generously with baste and place on grill. Barbecue, basting and turning often, for 6 to 8 minutes per side.

Makes: 4 servings

PREPARATION: 12 MINUTES
GRILL: 16 MINUTES

INDOOR SIZZLE:
For oven broiling, see page 76.

KEBABS

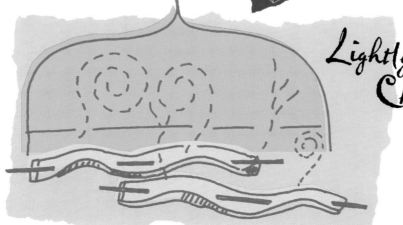

Lightly Curried Chicken Kebabs

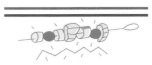

SOUTHWESTERN KEBABS

A simple mix of two store-bought sauces creates a lively blend of flavors.

Oil grill and preheat barbecue. Stir together
   3 tbsp salsa sauce
   3 tbsp plum sauce
Thread skewers with
   1 lb (500 g) beef sirloin or pork tenderloin, cut into 1½-inch (4-cm) pieces
   Generously brush with
   2 tbsp vegetable oil
Place skewers on grill and barbecue for 6 minutes, turning partway through. Then generously brush both sides of meat with sauce. Continue to grill, turning and basting often, until meat is done, about 4 minutes.
Makes: 4 servings

PREPARATION: 10 MINUTES
GRILL: 10 MINUTES

HAM-PINEAPPLE KEBABS

Remember these kebabs for a family gathering. They're always a winner, even with the most finicky kids.

Oil grill and preheat barbecue. Stir together
   3 tbsp brown sugar
   2 tbsp white vinegar
   1 tbsp vegetable oil
   1 tsp regular mustard
Thread skewers with
   ¾-lb (375-g) piece precooked ham, cut into 1-inch (2.5-cm) cubes
   alternating with
   14-oz can pineapple chunks, drained
Generously brush kebabs with baste. Place kebabs on grill. Barbecue with lid closed, turning and basting often, for 6 to 8 minutes, just until hot and richly glazed.
Makes: 3 to 4 servings

PREPARATION: 15 MINUTES
GRILL: 8 MINUTES

INDIAN LAMB KEBABS

Smother lamb in this quick, rich Indian-scented sauce that doesn't need cooking.

In a food processor, pulse together
   2 small onions, quartered
   ½ cup plain yogurt
   juice of 1 lemon
   3 garlic cloves
   1 tsp freshly ground black pepper
   ½ tsp turmeric
   ¼ tsp salt
   until onions are finely ground.
Trim and remove all visible fat and sinew from
   1 lb (500 g) boneless shoulder or leg of lamb, cut into 1-inch (2.5-cm) cubes
   Pour marinade over lamb cubes and toss until evenly coated. Cover and refrigerate for at least 1 hour, but no more than 4 hours. Stir mixture partway through marinating.
Oil grill and preheat barbecue. Thread marinated lamb cubes onto skewers, alternating with pieces of
   1 green pepper, seeded and cut into 1-inch (2.5-cm) pieces
   2 small onions, quartered
Discard marinade. Then generously brush lamb and vegetables with oil.
Place kebabs on grill and barbecue with lid closed, turning frequently, for about 4 to 5 minutes per side for medium.
Makes: 4 servings

PREPARATION: 15 MINUTES
MARINATE: 1 HOUR
GRILL: 10 MINUTES

ROSEMARY-ORANGE VEGETARIAN KEBABS

Wire up vegetarian hot dogs with an array of colorful vegetables and slather a simple rosemary-orange sauce over top for maximum flavor.

Thread alternately onto skewers
  2 peppers, sliced
    into 1-inch (2.5-cm) pieces
  2 small zucchini,
    sliced into 1-inch (2.5-cm) rounds
  20 small button mushrooms,
    stems trimmed
  20 cherry tomatoes, stems removed
  6 vegetarian hot dogs, preferably chili-
    flavored, sliced into 1-inch (2.5-cm) pieces
Oil grill and preheat barbecue. Whisk together
  ¼ cup frozen orange juice concentrate
  ¼ cup vegetable oil
  ¼ cup teriyaki sauce (optional)
  1 tsp dried rosemary, crushed
  1 tsp dried leaf oregano
  ½ tsp dried leaf thyme

Generously brush kebabs with mixture. Place on grill and barbecue until vegetables begin to brown, about 15 minutes. Turn often and brush with marinade. Serve with a crisp green salad with a creamy garlic dressing or wrap a bun around kebab and remove threaded skewer.

Makes: 6 servings

PREPARATION: 15 MINUTES
GRILL: 15 MINUTES

ROSEMARY-ORANGE VEGETARIAN KEBABS

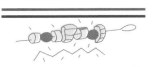

KEBABS

TENDER GARLIC LAMB KEBABS

Apple juice is a superb marinade which tenderizes lamb without overpowering its seductive taste.

Trim fat from
  8 lamb shoulder chops or 1½ lbs (750 g)
    boneless lamb
Remove meat from bones and cut into 1½-inch
  (4-cm) cubes. In a bowl or large self-sealing
  bag, combine
  1 cup apple juice or white wine
  ¼ cup soy sauce
  2 tbsp olive oil
  8 crushed garlic cloves
  2 tsp dried rosemary, crushed
  ¼ tsp black or cayenne pepper
  Add meat and stir, or manipulate bag, until
  well coated. Leave at room temperature for
  1 hour or refrigerate, preferably overnight.
Oil grill and preheat barbecue. Thread meat
  onto skewers and barbecue for about 8 to 10
  minutes, turning meat often and basting with
  marinade. Wonderful with simple baked
  potatoes or rice tossed with fresh mint.
Makes: 4 servings

PREPARATION: 20 MINUTES
MARINATE: 1 HOUR
GRILL: 10 MINUTES

INDOOR SIZZLE:
For oven broiling, see page 76.

MOROCCAN FISH KEBABS

Use our Moroccan all-purpose seasoning for any firm-fleshed fish that is a good buy.

Stir together
  ½ cup freshly squeezed lemon juice
  ⅓ cup olive oil
  6 crushed garlic cloves
  1 cup finely chopped fresh coriander
    or parsley
  1 tbsp paprika
  2 tsp ground cumin
  ½ tsp salt
  ½ tsp cayenne pepper
Thread onto skewers, leaving a little space
  between pieces
  1½ lbs (750 g) monkfish or other firm-fleshed
    fish, cut into 2-inch (5-cm) squares
Place in a single layer in a glass dish, just large
  enough to hold them snugly. Pour marinade
  over fish. Baste, making sure all pieces are
  coated. Cover and refrigerate for at least
  30 minutes. Turn skewers at least once during
  marinating and spoon sauce over top.
Oil grill and preheat barbecue. Drain fish and
  discard marinade. Grill fish until lightly
  golden, turning every 3 to 4 minutes, for
  15 to 20 minutes. Serve right away.
Makes: 4 to 6 servings

PREPARATION: 15 MINUTES
MARINATE: 30 MINUTES
GRILL: 20 MINUTES

Moroccan Fish Kebabs

FISH BROCHETTES

Here's a light yet substantial entrée that capitalizes on heart-healthy olive oil and fish steaks.

Stir together
　½ cup olive oil
　⅓ cup freshly squeezed lime juice
　¼ cup finely chopped fresh ginger
　2 tsp sugar
　½ tsp salt
　¼ tsp cayenne pepper
　freshly ground black pepper
　Thread skewers with
　1 box cherry tomatoes
　alternating with pieces of
　1 lb (500 g) swordfish, halibut or firm-fleshed
　　fish steaks, cut into 1-inch (2.5-cm) cubes
　3 small unpeeled zucchini,
　　sliced into ½-inch (1-cm) rounds
Oil grill and preheat barbecue. Liberally brush
　kebabs with olive oil mixture, making sure all
　surface area is coated. Grill, turning and
　basting frequently, until fish is cooked and
　vegetables are hot, about 10 minutes.
Makes: 4 servings

PREPARATION: 15 MINUTES
GRILL: 10 MINUTES

INDOOR SIZZLE:
For oven broiling, see page 76.

HALIBUT LIME KEBABS

This easy baste creates a succulent delicate taste with Mediterranean overtones.

Oil grill and preheat barbecue. Whisk together
　finely grated peel and juice of 1 lemon or lime
　finely grated peel and juice of 1 orange
　2 tbsp vegetable oil
　1 large crushed garlic clove
　½ tsp leaf oregano
Thread skewers with
　4 halibut steaks, about ½ lb (250 g) each,
　　cut into 1-inch (2.5-cm) chunks
　alternating with pieces of
　2 medium-size zucchini,
　　sliced into ½-inch (1-cm) rounds
　2 oranges, cut into ¼-inch (0.5-cm)
　　slices and halved
Brush kebabs with citrus mixture and barbecue
　for about 12 to 14 minutes, brushing with
　remaining marinade and turning frequently.
Makes: 4 to 6 servings

PREPARATION: 15 MINUTES
GRILL: 14 MINUTES

INDOOR SIZZLE:
For oven broiling, see page 76.

KEBABS

Fish Brochettes

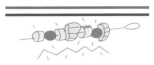

KEBABS

SAUSAGE KEBABS

If you're a sausage lover, here's the trick to dress them up for economical entertaining.

Preheat barbecue. In a small bowl, stir together
   ¼ cup olive oil
   1 tbsp dried basil
   1½ tsp dried leaf oregano
   pinch of salt
   generous grinding of black pepper
Thread skewers with
   1 lb (500 g) kielbasa, bratwurst or Italian
      sausage, cut into 1-inch (2.5-cm) pieces
   alternating with
   2 large sweet peppers,
      preferably 1 red and 1 green, seeded
      and cut into 1-inch (2.5-cm) pieces
   3 small zucchini,
      sliced into ½-inch (1-cm) rounds
Generously brush kebabs with basil baste.
   Then barbecue, covered, for 10 to 15 minutes,
   brushing with baste and turning occasionally.
   Some sausages just need warming, while
   Italian sausage needs thorough cooking.
   Serve over rice with naan bread or wrapped
   in tortillas.
Makes: 4 to 6 servings

PREPARATION: 15 MINUTES
GRILL: 15 MINUTES

INDOOR SIZZLE:
For oven broiling, see page 76.

EGGPLANT KEBABS

Use small cylindrical Japanese eggplants, which are tender and less bitter than regular eggplants.

Slice
   2 slim Japanese eggplants
   into ½-inch (1-cm) rounds
Generously brush with
   Italian salad dressing
Thread onto skewers and barbecue, covered,
   turning often, until golden, about
   15 minutes.
Makes: 4 servings

PREPARATION: 5 MINUTES
GRILL: 15 MINUTES

GARDEN VEGETABLE KEBABS

These pretty vegetable kebabs are perfect with a simple steak — whether it's a rib eye or tuna.

Thread alternately onto skewers, leaving a small
   space between each vegetable
   4 small green and yellow zucchini, sliced into
      1-inch (2.5-cm) pieces or rounds
   2 large sweet peppers, seeded and
      cut into 1-inch (2.5-cm) pieces
   1 box cherry tomatoes
Preheat barbecue. In a small dish, whisk together
   2 tbsp freshly squeezed lemon juice
   1 tbsp melted butter
   1 tsp dried basil
   generous pinches of salt and
      freshly ground black pepper
Liberally brush butter mixture over kebabs and
   place on grill. Barbecue, turning often and
   brushing with marinade, until vegetables
   begin to brown, about 10 to 15 minutes.
Makes: 4 servings

PREPARATION: 15 MINUTES
GRILL: 15 MINUTES

GOLDEN POTATO KEBABS

You'll want to make these addictive grilled potatoes again and again.
It's the highly seasoned olive oil baste that makes the difference.

Peel and slice in half lengthwise
4 baking potatoes
Precook by placing on a paper towel in the microwave and cooking on high for 6 to 8 minutes. Or bake at 350°F (180°C) for 30 minutes. Potatoes should still be fairly firm. Cut into rounds, about 1 inch (2.5 cm) thick, for easy skewering.
Place potatoes in a bowl. Drizzle with
olive oil

Liberally sprinkle with
pinches of salt, black pepper, cayenne pepper and cumin or chili powder
Stir until coated.
Thread potatoes onto skewers. You may need to thread two skewers through the potato pieces. Barbecue until potatoes are golden, about 20 to 25 minutes. Turn kebabs often and baste with more oil if they become dry.
Makes: 4 servings

PREPARATION: 10 MINUTES
MICROWAVE: 8 MINUTES
GRILL: 25 MINUTES

TIPS

BBQ Kebab Basics

• When making kebabs, make sure pieces are fairly even in size or you'll wind up with some sections charred or undercooked.

• Don't overcook small items. Chicken kebabs need about 10 minutes on a hot grill. Chicken is done when it feels firm.

• To avoid bacteria contamination, chicken kebabs should only be basted with a marinade for the first 2 minutes of barbecuing.

• Group together items on skewers which need the same amount of cooking. For example, group all the meat together and all the vegetables together.

• Leave space between the pieces on a kebab so they can brown on all sides. If meat cubes are pushed together, the sides pressed against one another will steam rather than barbecue.

Skewer Smarts

Here are tips to help add sizzle — and avoid seething over burnt offerings:

• Wooden skewers are a great inexpensive boon when serving a crowd. To avoid splintering when skewering and burning when barbecuing, soak skewers in warm water for at least 20 minutes. Then arrange food on skewers so that most of the wood is covered.

• Metal skewers speed up cooking by conducting heat into the middle of the food. Skewers at least 12 inches (30 cm) long with a good-size finial at one end are easy to grasp and the finials can be positioned outside the grill.

• Oval skewers, which are a deterrent to spinning food, are a better choice than round-shaped skewers.

*Succulent PROVENÇAL LAMB (see recipe page 90)
takes 30 minutes grilling and is perfect for a party.
A boneless leg of lamb, simply bathed in white wine,
garlic, rosemary and thyme, needs only
a single turning on the barbecue.*

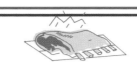

LAMB

ROSEMARY-PEPPER LAMB CHOPS

With little effort, you can add French-country flavor to succulent lamb chops.

Oil grill and preheat barbecue. Trim excess fat from
   8 lamb chops,
      each about 1 inch (2.5 cm) thick
Stir together
   2 tbsp olive oil
   1 tsp freshly ground black pepper
   1 tsp dried rosemary, crushed
   2 crushed garlic cloves
   ¼ tsp salt
Rub into both sides of chops.
Place chops on grill and barbecue until lamb is cooked as you like it, about 4 to 7 minutes per side for medium-rare chops. Serve with grilled potatoes and vegetables, and Tomato & Hot Pepper Salsa (see recipe page 111).
Makes: 4 servings

PREPARATION: 5 MINUTES
GRILL: 14 MINUTES

INDOOR SIZZLE:
For oven broiling, see below.

MOROCCAN CHOPS

Here's a fast way to create an aromatic Moroccan baste for tender lamb chops.

In a small bowl, whisk together
   ¼ cup olive or vegetable oil
   1 crushed garlic clove
      or ½ tsp bottled minced garlic
   1 tsp curry powder
   ¼ tsp cinnamon
   ¼ tsp cardamom
Trim excess fat from
   8 lamb chops, each about 1 inch (2.5 cm) thick
Place in a single layer in a glass dish or a self-sealing bag. Pour marinade over lamb chops. Turn chops once or twice to coat. Cover dish or seal bag and leave at room temperature for 1 hour or refrigerate for at least 2 hours or overnight.
Oil grill and preheat barbecue. When hot, place drained marinated lamb on grill. Barbecue for 4 to 7 minutes per side for medium-rare. Serve with couscous.
Makes: 4 servings

PREPARATION: 5 MINUTES
MARINATE: 1 HOUR
GRILL: 14 MINUTES

INDOOR SIZZLE:
For oven broiling, see below.

INDOOR BROILING FOR YEAR-ROUND SIZZLE

Where a recipe indicates Indoor Sizzle, prepare lamb as directed, but when it's time to barbecue, use this oven method instead. Preheat broiler. Place oven rack so top of lamb is at least 4 inches (10 cm) from broiler. Place leg of lamb on a rack in a shallow baking pan. Broil for 10 minutes per side for medium-rare. Broil chops for 4 to 6 minutes per side.

GARLIC-ROSEMARY LAMB CHOPS

The combination of fresh lemon juice, garlic and rosemary is a great natural tenderizer in this superb lamb marinade.

In a large bowl, whisk together
- ⅓ cup olive oil
- ¼ cup freshly squeezed lemon juice
- 4 crushed garlic cloves
- 1 tsp cracked or coarsely ground black peppercorns
- 4 sprigs fresh rosemary, chopped

Place in marinade
- 3 lbs (1.5 kg) lamb chops, each at least 1 inch (2.5 cm) thick

and turn to coat. Cover and leave at room temperature for 1 hour or refrigerate at least 2 hours or overnight. Turn at least once during this time.

Remove from refrigerator about 1 hour before barbecuing to bring to room temperature. Oil grill and preheat barbecue. Remove chops from marinade and barbecue about 5 minutes per side for medium-rare.

Makes: 6 servings

PREPARATION: 15 MINUTES
MARINATE: 1 HOUR
GRILL: 10 MINUTES

INDOOR SIZZLE:
For oven broiling, see page 88.

GARLIC-ROSEMARY LAMB CHOPS

LAMB

PROVENÇAL LAMB

Here's an easy party roast that only needs one turning on the barbie.

Trim excess fat from
 3½-lb (1.75-kg) boneless leg of lamb
 and place in a shallow dish just large enough
 to snugly hold it or in a large self-sealing bag.
Whisk together
 1½ cups dry white wine
 ¼ cup olive oil
 6 crushed garlic cloves
 2 tsp dried rosemary
 1 tsp leaf thyme
 1 tsp coarsely ground black pepper
 ½ tsp cayenne pepper (optional)
 Pour over lamb. Cover or seal bag. Leave at
 room temperature for 1 hour or refrigerate
 for several hours or overnight. Turn lamb at
 least once during this time. Remove from
 refrigerator about 1 hour before barbecuing.
Oil grill and preheat barbecue. Discard
 marinade and place lamb on barbecue. Close
 lid or cover with a foil tent. Barbecue 10 to
 15 minutes per side until lamb feels springy.
 Let stand, covered, for 10 minutes before
 slicing. Serve with big bowls of ratatouille,
 fresh green peas and tiny new potatoes.
Makes: 8 servings

PREPARATION: 10 MINUTES
MARINATE: 1 HOUR
GRILL: 30 MINUTES

INDOOR SIZZLE:
For oven broiling, see page 88.

MEDITERRANEAN LAMB

Lusty red wine lends its fruity taste to this herbed marinade. Marvelous with garlic mashed potatoes.

Whisk together
 ½ cup dry red wine
 ¼ cup olive or vegetable oil
 2 crushed garlic cloves
 1 tbsp dried leaf oregano
 1 tbsp rosemary, crushed
 ½ tsp freshly ground black pepper
Trim excess fat from
 3½-lb (1.75-kg) butterflied boneless leg
 of lamb
 and place in a shallow dish just large enough
 to hold it snugly or in a self-sealing bag. Pour
 wine mixture over lamb, turning until evenly
 coated. Cover or seal and leave at room
 temperature for 1 hour or refrigerate for at
 least 4 hours, preferably overnight. Turn meat
 at least twice during this time.
Oil grill and preheat barbecue. Remove lamb
 from marinade and place on grill. If lamb is
 1½ inches (4 cm) thick, barbecue for 10 to
 15 minutes per side for medium doneness.
 If 3 inches (8 cm) thick, barbecue for 18 to
 20 minutes per side. Remove lamb to a
 cutting board or platter and let stand at least
 5 minutes before slicing diagonally.
Makes: 4 servings

PREPARATION: 10 MINUTES
MARINATE: 1 HOUR
GRILL: 40 MINUTES

INDOOR SIZZLE:
For oven broiling, see page 88.

LAMB WITH FRESH MINT VINAIGRETTE

The traditional lamb and mint are still a knockout combination.
Here's an exciting new way to join them.

Oil grill and preheat barbecue. Trim excess fat from
8 small lamb chops,
    each about 1 inch (2.5 cm) thick
Grill chops about 4 to 7 minutes per side for medium-rare.
Meanwhile, whisk together
    ⅓ cup olive or vegetable oil
    1 tbsp freshly squeezed lemon juice
    finely grated peel of 1 lemon
    1 crushed garlic clove
    generous pinches of salt and
        freshly ground black pepper

Stir in
¼ cup finely chopped fresh mint
Place hot grilled chops on platter. Spoon mint vinaigrette over top and serve.
Makes: 4 servings

PREPARATION: 15 MINUTES
GRILL: 14 MINUTES

INDOOR SIZZLE:
For oven broiling, see page 88.

LAMB WITH FRESH MINT VINAIGRETTE

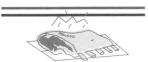

LAMB

FRENCH GRILLED LEG OF LAMB

In half an hour you can produce a leg of lamb that rivals the finest French bistro offering.

Oil grill and preheat barbecue. Trim excess fat and skin from
  3½-lb (1.75-kg) boneless leg of lamb
In a medium-size bowl, whisk together
  ¼ cup Dijon mustard
  ¼ cup white wine
  2 tbsp vegetable oil
  1 tbsp Worcestershire sauce
  2 crushed garlic cloves
  ½ tsp granulated sugar
  ½ tsp freshly ground black pepper
Massage mixture into both sides of meat.
Barbecue for about 8 to 10 minutes per side for rare lamb, brushing with mustard mixture. Remove lamb to a cutting board or platter and let stand 5 minutes before slicing diagonally. Serve with garlic mashed potatoes.
Makes: 6 servings

PREPARATION: 10 MINUTES
GRILL: 20 MINUTES

INDOOR SIZZLE: *Oven Broiling*
Place meat on a broiler rack. Massage half the mixture into meat. Position about 4 inches (10 cm) from preheated broiler. Broil for 8 minutes. Turn meat and massage remaining mixture into meat. Continue to broil for 5 to 8 more minutes for rare.

MINT & GARLIC LEG OF LAMB

Garlic and fresh mint can always be counted on to create an outstanding marriage with lamb.

In a large bowl, whisk together
  ¼ cup olive or vegetable oil
  ¼ cup freshly squeezed lemon juice
  3 crushed garlic cloves
  ½ tsp cracked black pepper
Add
  3-lb (1.5-kg) boneless leg of lamb
Sprinkle with
  ⅔ cup shredded mint leaves
Turn to coat.
Cover and leave at room temperature for at least 1 hour or refrigerate overnight. Turn at least once, but remove from refrigerator about 1 hour before barbecuing.
Oil grill and preheat barbecue. Remove lamb from marinade and place on grill. If lamb is 1½ inches (4 cm) thick, barbecue for 10 to 15 minutes per side for medium doneness. If 3 inches (8 cm) thick, barbecue for 18 to 20 minutes per side. Remove lamb to a cutting board or platter and let stand at least 5 minutes before slicing diagonally. This marinade is also wonderful with chicken and beef.
Makes: 8 to 10 servings

PREPARATION: 15 MINUTES
MARINATE: 1 HOUR
GRILL: 40 MINUTES

SESAME-MUSTARD LAMB

Sesame oil packs such an intriguing smoky taste, it's no wonder people are wild for it.
For this baste, simply stir it with mustard and honey.

Oil grill and preheat barbecue. With a sharp
  knife, remove silverskin from
  1½-lb (750-g) pkg lamb loins
    or 6 loin lamb chops
  (The silverskin is the thin membrane found
  on one side of the lamb loin.)
In a small bowl, whisk together
  ¼ cup vegetable or dark sesame oil
  ¼ cup coarse-grained mustard
  2 tbsp liquid honey

Brush over lamb. Place on grill and barbecue
  for about 4 to 7 minutes per side for
  medium-rare, turning frequently and
  brushing with remaining mustard mixture.
Makes: 4 servings

PREPARATION: 5 MINUTES
GRILL: 16 MINUTES

Sesame-Mustard Lamb

TIPS

BBQ Lamb Basics

- Marinades add extra flavor and moistness and tenderize lamb. But they often call for large quantities of fat. If you marinate lamb in white wine or apple juice mixed with herbs for at least 4 hours or overnight, the liquid will be absorbed and the lamb will be wonderfully moist with no extra oil needed.

- Instead of basting the food with oil throughout barbecuing, just lightly brush the outside of lamb with oil before placing it on the grill.

- To ensure even cooking and avoid overcooking, bring chops to room temperature before grilling.

- To prevent sticking, oil the grill before you turn on the barbecue. If you brush a hot grill, it can melt the brush, and if oil drips on coals, it may flare. Or instead of oiling the grill before heating, coat with a nonstick cooking spray.

- To prevent curling, trim fat from lamb chops and nick edges.

- A leg of lamb works beautifully on the barbecue. Boneless legs work best. Position the thinnest portion over the coolest side of the grill. If cooking a leg with the bone-in, do over a medium heat with the lid closed, turning often.

Pork steaks are a great way to stretch your steak dollar,
but look anything but budget here. SMOKY APPLE STEAKS
(top, see recipe page 98) are bathed in a chili-apple baste, while
SAGE-SCENTED PORK STEAKS (see recipe page 96)
are treated to a delicious lusty sage-and-garlic marinade.

PORK

SAGE-SCENTED PORK STEAKS

Fresh sage and balsamic vinegar give a double punch of flavor to these meaty yet light steaks.

Whisk together
⅓ cup olive or vegetable oil
¼ cup balsamic or red wine vinegar
2 tbsp finely chopped fresh sage
1 crushed garlic clove
½ tsp freshly ground black pepper

Place
4 pork steaks, each about
1 inch (2.5 cm) thick
in a shallow dish just large enough to hold them snugly or in a self-sealing bag. Pour marinade over top.

Cover or seal and leave at room temperature for 1 hour or refrigerate overnight. Turn steaks partway through marinating. Before barbecuing, remove dish from refrigerator and bring steaks to room temperature.

Oil grill and preheat barbecue. Remove steaks from marinade. Place on grill and barbecue for about 8 minutes, then turn. Continue barbecuing for about 5 to 8 more minutes.

Makes: 4 to 6 servings

PREPARATION: 15 MINUTES
MARINATE: 1 HOUR
GRILL: 16 MINUTES

INDOOR SIZZLE:
For oven broiling, see below.

ORANGE-PEPPER PORK CHOPS

With very little effort and ingredients already on hand, you can grill up these zesty satisfying chops.

Whisk together
finely grated peel of 1 orange
¼ cup orange juice
¼ cup white wine
2 tbsp olive or vegetable oil
¼ cup chopped shallots
or 2 crushed garlic cloves
½ tsp cracked black peppercorns

Place
4 pork chops
in a shallow dish just large enough to hold them snugly or in a self-sealing bag. Pour marinade over top. Turn chops once or twice to coat. Cover or seal and refrigerate for at least 1 hour or overnight. Turn halfway through.

Oil grill and preheat barbecue. Remove chops from marinade and place on grill. Cover with barbecue lid or foil tent. Barbecue for 4 to 6 minutes per side for ½-inch (1-cm) thick chops.

Makes: 4 servings

PREPARATION: 15 MINUTES
MARINATE: 1 HOUR
GRILL: 12 MINUTES

INDOOR SIZZLE:
For oven broiling, see below.

INDOOR BROILING FOR YEAR-ROUND SIZZLE

Where a recipe indicates Indoor Sizzle, prepare pork as directed, but when it's time to barbecue, use this oven method instead. Preheat broiler. Set pork on a rack on a baking sheet with shallow sides. Place at least 4 inches (10 cm) from preheated broiler. Broil for 6 to 8 minutes per side. For kebabs, thread marinated pork onto skewers and continue as above.

FIERY PORK SKEWERS

Teriyaki sauce gives an Asian touch to these fast kebabs.
Great on a bed of rice with grilled tomatoes.

Oil grill and preheat barbecue. In a small bowl, stir together

2 tbsp teriyaki sauce
1 tbsp red wine vinegar
1 tbsp vegetable oil
1 tsp brown sugar
¼ tsp hot red pepper flakes

Pour mixture over

1 pork tenderloin, about ¾ lb (375 g), cut into 1-inch (2.5-cm) cubes

Toss to coat.

Thread meat onto skewers. Place on hot grill and barbecue, turning often and brushing with sauce, until pork is done as you like, about 10 to 12 minutes.

Makes: 4 servings

PREPARATION: 15 MINUTES
GRILL: 12 MINUTES

INDOOR SIZZLE:
For oven broiling, see page 96.

FIERY PORK SKEWERS

SMOKY APPLE STEAKS

*Deliver a very smoky taste with liquid smoke.
Look for it in small jars in the supermarket.*

Stir together
 ½ cup apple juice
 ½ cup barbecue sauce
 ¼ cup cider vinegar
 ¼ tsp liquid smoke
 ¼ tsp hot red pepper flakes
Place
 4 pork steaks, each about
  1 inch (2.5 cm) thick
in a shallow dish just large enough to hold
them snugly or in a self-sealing bag. Pour
sauce over steaks. Turn several times until
well coated.
Cover or seal and leave at room temperature for
 1 hour or refrigerate overnight. Turn steaks
 partway through marinating.
Oil grill and preheat barbecue. Place steaks on
 grill. Discard marinade. Barbecue with lid
 closed for 8 minutes, then turn. Continue
 barbecuing for 5 to 8 more minutes. To test
 doneness, press centre of each steak with your
 finger. They should feel fairly firm
 throughout. Serve steaks with apple wedges
 or halves that you've grilled on the barbie
 along with the pork.
Makes: 4 servings

PREPARATION: 15 MINUTES
MARINATE: 1 HOUR
GRILL: 16 MINUTES

INDOOR SIZZLE:
For oven broiling, see page 96.

BUTTERFLIED TANDOORI CHOPS

*This yogurt marinade is so full of flavor you
only have to marinate for an hour.*

Trim fat from edges of
 4 boneless butterflied loin pork chops,
  each about ¾ inch (2 cm) thick
In a food processor, whirl until finely chopped
 1 small onion, quartered
 1 garlic clove
 1-inch (2.5-cm) piece peeled fresh ginger
 1 jalapeño pepper, seeded
 2 tbsp freshly squeezed lemon juice
 1 tsp curry or garam masala
 ½ tsp salt
Add
 6-oz (175-mL) container plain yogurt,
  about ¾ cup
and whirl until smooth.
Place chops in a self-sealing bag and pour in
 yogurt mixture so it coats meat evenly.
 Seal and refrigerate for at least 1 hour, or
 preferably overnight for best flavor, turning
 bag once.
Oil grill and preheat barbecue. Place chops on
 grill. Barbecue with the lid closed, turning
 once, until browned and chops feel firm to
 the touch, about 12 to 15 minutes. Serve with
 rice or couscous mixed with lots of chopped
 chives and a broccoli-and-red pepper salad.
Makes: 4 servings

PREPARATION: 15 MINUTES
MARINATE: 1 HOUR
GRILL: 15 MINUTES

INDOOR SIZZLE:
For oven broiling, see page 96.

HONG KONG PORK

Pantry staples combine to give an Oriental kick to lean pork tenderloins.

Oil grill and preheat barbecue. Whisk together
   2 tbsp chili sauce
   2 tbsp liquid honey
   2 tbsp soy sauce
   2 crushed garlic cloves
   ½ tsp ground ginger
Brush mixture over
   2 pork tenderloins, each about ¾ lb (375 g)
   Place tenderloins on grill and barbecue for 15 to 20 minutes, turning and basting often.
   Makes: 6 servings

PREPARATION: 5 MINUTES
GRILL: 20 MINUTES

HERBED DIJON TENDERLOINS

Round out these delicious tenderloins with an avocado salad, grilled peppers and zucchini.

Oil grill and preheat barbecue. Whisk together
   2 tbsp Dijon mustard, preferably
      coarse-grained
   2 tsp vegetable oil
   1 tsp leaf thyme
   ½ tsp dried rosemary, crushed
   ¼ tsp coarsely ground black pepper
Generously spread mixture over
   2 pork tenderloins, each about ¾ lb (375 g)
   Place on grill and barbecue for 15 to 20 minutes, turning and basting often.
   Makes: 6 servings

PREPARATION: 5 MINUTES
GRILL: 20 MINUTES

PORK

TIPS

BBQ Pork Basics

- Marinades add extra flavor and moistness and tenderize pork. But they often call for large quantities of fat. If you marinate pork in white wine, apple juice or cider mixed with herbs and a little soy sauce for at least 4 hours or overnight, the liquid will be absorbed and the pork will be wonderfully moist with no oil needed.

- Instead of basting the food with oil throughout barbecuing, just lightly brush the outside of pork with oil before placing it on the grill.

- Instead of oiling the grill before heating, coat with a nonstick cooking spray.

- Partially cook pork chops in the microwave, then finish on the grill.

- To ensure even cooking, bring chops to room temperature before grilling.

- Don't overcook pork. It's wonderful cooked just until pink in the centre. (At one time, we had to overcook pork until it was well-done to destroy trichinosis, but this has been virtually non-existent in Canada for more than 10 years due to improved production methods.)

CLASSIC BARBECUE RIBS (see recipe page 106) glazed with a thick homemade sauce are a sure winner with every age group. Add a potato salad and corn on the cob for a true old-fashioned feast.

RIBS

CAN'T-BE-BEAT RIBS

Creating an old-fashioned barbecue sauce is worth the effort for these outstanding ribs.

Trim excess fat from
   6 lbs (3 kg) back ribs
Then precook ribs (see Tips page 107).
Stir together
   1 cup each ketchup and chili sauce
   ⅔ cup vegetable oil
   ¼ cup brown sugar
   2 tbsp Worcestershire sauce
   2 tsp dry mustard
      or ¼ cup regular prepared mustard
   1 tsp each cayenne pepper and garlic powder
Drain precooked ribs well and cut into serving-
   size pieces, about 3 to 4 ribs per section.
Oil grill and preheat barbecue. Brush ribs with
   sauce. Place ribs on hot grill and barbecue
   for 5 minutes, then turn. Continue basting
   often with remaining sauce and turning until
   ribs are richly glazed and heated through,
   about 10 to 15 more minutes. Serve extra
   sauce for dipping.
Makes: 6 to 8 servings

PREPARATION: 10 MINUTES
COOK: 1 HOUR
GRILL: 20 MINUTES

INDOOR SIZZLE:
For oven baking, see below.

CANADIAN ORIENTAL RIBS

After you've cooked up these ribs you'll wonder why you hadn't used a maple syrup base before.

Trim excess fat from
   3 to 4 lbs (1.5 to 2 kg) back ribs
Then precook ribs (see Tips page 107).
In a medium-size saucepan, stir together
   ½ cup pure maple syrup
   ¼ cup sherry
   2 tbsp each vegetable oil and soy sauce
   2 crushed garlic cloves
   1 to 2 tbsp finely grated fresh ginger
Bring to a boil over medium heat and boil gently,
   uncovered and stirring often, for 5 minutes to
   develop flavors.
Drain precooked ribs well and cut into serving-
   size pieces, about 3 to 4 ribs per section.
Oil grill and preheat barbecue. Brush ribs with
   maple syrup mixture. Place coated ribs on
   grill and barbecue, turning ribs every
   5 minutes and basting with remaining maple
   syrup mixture, until heated through, about
   15 to 20 minutes.
Makes: 4 to 6 servings

PREPARATION: 10 MINUTES
COOK: 1 HOUR
GRILL: 20 MINUTES

INDOOR SIZZLE:
For oven baking, see below.

INDOOR BAKING FOR YEAR-ROUND SIZZLE

Where a recipe indicates Indoor Sizzle, prepare ribs as directed, but when it's time to barbecue, use this oven method instead. Place basted precooked ribs on a rack set in a shallow-sided pan. Cook in a preheated 425°F (220°C) oven, turning often and basting, just until ribs are hot and glazed.

CAJUN-COATED RIBS

Create a fire-and-spice dry coating with this "secret mix" of everyday spices.

Trim excess fat from
  4 lbs (2 kg) back ribs
Then precook ribs (see Tips page 107).
Stir together
  2 tbsp paprika
  1 tbsp coarsely ground black pepper
  1 ½ tsp garlic salt
  1 ½ tsp onion salt
  ½ tsp cayenne pepper
Drain precooked ribs well and cut into serving-
  size pieces, about 3 to 4 ribs per section (or
  more, if doing a lot of ribs at once on the grill).
Oil grill and preheat barbecue. Brush ribs with
  vegetable oil

Lay ribs on a piece of waxed paper or a plate.
  Thickly coat each side with seasoning
  mixture and rub in. Place on grill and
  barbecue, turning occasionally, until
  browned and cooked as you like, about
  20 to 25 minutes. Serve with Sweet 'n' Sour
  Cucumber Salsa (see recipe page 110) and
  a cooling yogurt smoothie.
Makes: 4 to 6 servings

PREPARATION: 15 MINUTES
COOK: 1 HOUR
GRILL: 25 MINUTES

INDOOR SIZZLE:
For oven baking, see page 102.

CAJUN-COATED RIBS

RIBS

TEX-MEX SPARERIBS

*Big fiery taste comes from a bottle of taco sauce
laced with a cluster of garlic.*

Trim excess fat from
    3 to 4 lbs (1.5 to 2 kg) back ribs
Then precook ribs (see Tips page 107).
Stir together
    8-oz (250-mL) bottle or 1 cup taco sauce
    ¼ cup vegetable oil
    6 crushed garlic cloves
    2 tbsp ground cumin
Drain precooked ribs well and cut into serving-
    size pieces, about 3 to 4 ribs per section.
Oil grill and preheat barbecue. Generously
    brush ribs with sauce. Place coated ribs on
    grill and barbecue for 5 minutes, then turn
    and brush with sauce. Continue basting and
    turning until ribs are richly glazed and heated
    through, about 10 to 15 more minutes.
Makes: 4 servings

> *PREPARATION: 10 MINUTES*
> *COOK: 1 HOUR*
> *GRILL: 20 MINUTES*

CHILI-RUBBED RIBS

*Never underestimate ketchup. It's the perfect
sweet-sour base for powerfully flavored ribs.*

Trim excess fat from
    5 lbs (2.5 kg) pork side ribs
Then precook ribs (see Tips page 107).
Whisk together
    ¼ cup ketchup
    2 tbsp vegetable oil
    2 tbsp Worcestershire sauce
    6 crushed garlic cloves
    2 tbsp chili powder
    1 tbsp brown sugar
    2 tsp ground cumin (optional)
Drain precooked ribs well and cut into serving-
    size pieces, about 3 to 4 ribs per section.

Oil grill and preheat barbecue. Place cooked ribs
on hot grill and barbecue for 5 minutes per
side. Then generously brush sauce over both
sides of ribs. Continue barbecuing until ribs
are richly glazed, about 3 to 4 more minutes
per side. Serve any remaining sauce on the
side for dipping. Terrific with potato salad.
Makes: 6 to 8 servings

> *PREPARATION: 10 MINUTES*
> *COOK: 1 HOUR*
> *GRILL: 18 MINUTES*

INDOOR SIZZLE:
For oven baking, see page 102.

KOREAN BEEF RIBS

*If you love the ribs from a roast because of the
delicious browned areas, these ribs will deliver.*

Trim excess fat from
    3 lbs (1.5 kg) beef short ribs, about 8 pieces
Then precook ribs (see Tips page 107, but
    cook only 30 minutes).
Whisk together
    ½ cup each vegetable oil and soy sauce
    ¼ cup brown sugar
    4 crushed garlic cloves
    2 tbsp curry powder
Drain precooked ribs well and cut into serving-
    size pieces, about 3 to 4 ribs per section.
Oil grill and preheat barbecue. Place ribs on hot
    grill and barbecue for 5 minutes, then turn
    and brush with sauce. Continue basting and
    turning until ribs are richly glazed and heated
    through, about 10 to 15 more minutes.
Makes: 3 to 4 servings

> *PREPARATION: 15 MINUTES*
> *COOK: 30 MINUTES*
> *GRILL: 20 MINUTES*

INDOOR SIZZLE:
For oven baking, see page 102.

BLOODY MARY RIBS

This is the ultimate baste for Bloody Mary lovers. It gets a fast start from spicy store-bought juice.

Trim excess fat from
 4 lbs (2 kg) back ribs
Then precook ribs (see Tips page 107). Stir
 together
  1 cup vegetable juice cocktail mix, such as V-8
  ¼ cup vegetable oil
  1 tbsp each horseradish, freshly squeezed
    lemon juice and regular prepared mustard
  2 tsp Worcestershire sauce
  1 tsp hot pepper sauce
  ½ tsp freshly ground black pepper
Drain precooked ribs well and cut into serving-
 size pieces, about 3 to 4 ribs per section.
 Arrange ribs in a shallow dish just large
 enough to hold them snugly or place in a
 self-sealing bag. Pour Bloody Mary sauce

over ribs, turning to ensure ribs are coated.
Ribs can be cooked right away or covered and
refrigerated overnight before cooking.
Oil grill and preheat barbecue. Place coated ribs
on grill and barbecue for about 5 minutes,
then turn and brush with sauce. Continue
basting and turning ribs often until heated
through, about 10 to 15 more minutes.
Makes: 4 to 6 servings

PREPARATION: 10 MINUTES
COOK: 1 HOUR
GRILL: 20 MINUTES

INDOOR SIZZLE:
For oven baking, see page 102.

BLOODY MARY RIBS

RIBS

CLASSIC BARBECUED RIBS

Here's a fast way to deliver old-fashioned homemade taste to succulent ribs.

Trim excess fat from
    6 lbs (3 kg) back ribs
Then precook ribs (see Tips page 107).
In a medium-size saucepan, heat
    2 tbsp vegetable oil
    Add
    1 onion, finely chopped
    1 green pepper, finely chopped (optional)
    1 crushed garlic clove
    Sauté until onion is soft, about 5 minutes.
Stir in
    10-oz (285-mL) bottle chili sauce
    $\frac{1}{4}$ cup brown sugar
    2 tbsp cider vinegar
    1 tbsp Worcestershire sauce
    2 tsp dry mustard
    $\frac{1}{2}$ tsp hot pepper sauce
    pinch of cayenne pepper
    Simmer, covered, stirring often, for about 15 minutes to develop flavor.
Drain precooked ribs well and cut into serving-size pieces, about 3 to 4 ribs per section (or more, if doing a lot of ribs at once on the grill).
Oil grill and preheat barbecue. Generously brush ribs with sauce. Place coated ribs on hot grill and barbecue, turning ribs every 5 minutes and basting often with remaining sauce, until heated through, about 15 to 20 minutes. Serve remaining sauce for dipping.
Makes: 6 to 8 servings

PREPARATION: 10 MINUTES
COOK: 1 HOUR
GRILL: 20 MINUTES

INDOOR SIZZLE:
For oven baking, see page 102.

LUSCIOUS SMOKED RIBS

A smokehouse isn't needed to re-create those smoky ribs you probably fell in love with at a rib restaurant.

Trim excess fat from
    3 to 4 lbs (1.5 to 2 kg) back ribs
Then precook ribs (see Tips page 107).
In a large wide saucepan, heat
    $\frac{1}{4}$ cup vegetable oil
    Add
    1 large onion, chopped
    4 crushed garlic cloves
    Sauté over medium-low heat, stirring often, just until onion is soft, about 5 minutes.
    Add
    14-oz (398-mL) can or $1\frac{3}{4}$ cups crushed tomatoes
    $\frac{1}{2}$ cup each brown sugar and cider vinegar
    3 tbsp Worcestershire sauce
    2 tbsp regular prepared mustard
    1 tbsp liquid smoke
    2 tsp cayenne pepper
Bring to a boil, stirring often, until sugar is dissolved. Then boil gently, uncovered, stirring frequently, for about 10 minutes to develop flavors.
Drain precooked ribs well and cut into serving-size pieces, about 3 to 4 ribs per section (or more, if doing a lot of ribs at once on the grill).
Oil grill and preheat barbecue. Generously brush ribs with sauce. Place coated ribs on hot grill and barbecue, turning ribs every 5 minutes and basting often with remaining sauce, until heated through, about 15 to 20 minutes. Serve remaining sauce for dipping.
Makes: 4 to 6 servings

PREPARATION: 10 MINUTES
COOK: 1 HOUR
GRILL: 20 MINUTES

INDOOR SIZZLE:
For oven baking, see page 102.

CHRIS'S RACY RIBS

Simmer ribs directly in sauce instead of water to tenderize. Then either barbecue or broil.

Trim excess fat from
    2 to 3 lbs (1 to 1.5 kg) pork back ribs
In a large saucepan, combine
    ¼ cup ketchup
    ¼ cup soy sauce
    ¼ cup maple syrup, honey or brown sugar
    1½ cups water
    ½ tsp hot red pepper flakes (optional)
Add ribs and turn to coat with mixture. Bring
    sauce to a boil over high heat. Then reduce to
    low, cover and simmer until fork-tender, about
    50 minutes. Remove ribs. Increase heat to high
    and boil liquid, uncovered, until thickened like
    a barbecue sauce, about 20 to 25 minutes.

Watch carefully to avoid burning. Grill ribs over a medium-hot barbecue, basting with sauce, until hot and richly glazed, from 6 to 8 minutes per side. Serve sauce for dipping.
Makes: 2 to 3 servings

PREPARATION: 5 MINUTES
COOK: 1¼ HOURS
GRILL: 16 MINUTES

INDOOR SIZZLE: *Oven Broiling*
Preheat broiler. Broil ribs on a rack about 4 inches (10 cm) from broiler, basting often with sauce, about 6 to 8 minutes per side.

TIPS

Precooking Ribs

- Always precook ribs or they'll burn before becoming tender. Fold or cut racks in half and place in a large saucepan. Fill with enough water to cover ribs completely, then bring to a boil. Simmer, covered, until fork-tender, from 45 minutes to 1 hour. (If not using right away, wrap and refrigerate or freeze. Ribs will keep well in the refrigerator for 2 days.)

- Spareribs have a thin membrane running along the bony side. It shrinks during cooking, causing the ribs to curl, and remains tough and chewy. To remove, run a fork tine underneath the membrane and lift the fork to loosen. Grasp membrane firmly and pull. It should come off easily in one piece.

Buying Ribs

Most supermarkets stock three kinds of pork ribs — pork side ribs, pork back ribs and country style pork ribs.

- Side Ribs: These ribs, also called spareribs, have a large white flat bone and less meat than back or country style. While often the lowest price per pound, they deliver less meat.

- Back Ribs: These ribs have shorter bones and more meat than side ribs. Side or back ribs can be used interchangeably in recipes.

- Country Style Ribs: This is a pork loin roast with the ribs still attached. Often the most expensive rib, the meat can be tender enough that they don't have to be precooked in water. Barbecue with the lid closed over low heat.

Whether you're grilling a burger or expensive tuna steak,
colorful sauces or fresh salsas (a fancy name for relishes) give a
tremendous boost of fresh taste and texture. Clockwise from top:
TOMATO & HOT PEPPER SALSA, BLACK BEAN 'N' PEPPER SALSA,
SWEET 'N' SOUR CUCUMBER SALSA, STRAWBERRY & GINGER SALSA,
FRESH MINT & NECTARINE SALSA, ROASTED RED REPPER SAUCE
(see recipe pages 110 and 111).

STRAWBERRY & GINGER SALSA

Try this new twist on fruit salad with grilled chicken, pork or on cottage cheese.

In a small bowl, combine
    1 pint strawberries, sliced or chopped
    1 orange, peeled and finely chopped
    1 Granny Smith apple or green-skinned pear, cored and finely chopped
Then sprinkle with
    1 tbsp granulated sugar
    1 tbsp lemon juice
    1 tsp grated fresh ginger
    Gently toss.
    Taste and stir in more sugar and juice if needed. Salsa is best served the day it is made.
Makes: 3 cups

PREPARATION: 10 MINUTES

SWEET 'N' SOUR CUCUMBER SALSA

Lime and dill perk up cucumber as a cool companion for any fiery dish.

In a large bowl, combine
    ½ unpeeled English cucumber, diced
    1 sweet red pepper, finely chopped
    ½ cup finely chopped red onion
Stir in
    ½ cup chopped fresh dill
    3 tbsp freshly squeezed lime or lemon juice
    2 tbsp granulated sugar
    ¼ tsp salt
Use right away or cover and refrigerate for up to 1 day. It softens as it sits. Serve with Cajun-Coated Ribs (see recipe page 103) or Grilled Jerk Chicken (see recipe page 48).
Makes: 3 cups

PREPARATION: 10 MINUTES

ROASTED RED PEPPER SAUCE

Add a few peppers to the grill during your next barbecue, then whirl up this addictive sauce.

Oil grill and preheat barbecue. Grill
    4 large sweet red peppers
    turning often, until blackened and blistered on all sides, about 15 to 25 minutes. Place hot blackened peppers in a paper bag. Seal and let stand until peppers are cool enough to handle, about 10 minutes. Peel away skin. Then core and seed peppers.
In a food processor, whirl peppers until almost smooth with
    2 crushed garlic cloves
    ¼ cup coarsely chopped fresh basil
    ¼ tsp each of salt and pepper
Use right away or cover and refrigerate for up to 3 days or freeze. Good on everything from steak to fish.
Makes: 2 cups

PREPARATION: 15 MINUTES
GRILL: 25 MINUTES

INDOOR SIZZLE:
For oven broiling, see page 124.

FRESH MINT & NECTARINE SALSA

Plums and nectarines create an intriguing dress-up for chicken, lamb or fish steaks.

In a small bowl, combine
    3 nectarines, finely chopped
    2 plums, finely chopped
    Stir in
    2 to 4 tbsp finely chopped fresh mint
    2 tbsp liquid honey
    1 tbsp freshly squeezed lime or lemon juice
For fullest flavor, serve this salsa at room temperature on the same day it is made.
Makes: 3 cups

PREPARATION: 10 MINUTES

TOMATO & HOT PEPPER SALSA

Jazz up chopped fresh tomatoes with lots of garlic and hot pepper for a wallop of taste.

In a medium-size bowl, combine
    6 tomatoes, seeded and
      coarsely chopped
    2 green onions, thinly sliced

Stir in
    2 crushed garlic cloves
    1 to 2 tbsp seeded and finely chopped
      hot banana or jalapeño pepper
    1 tbsp olive oil
    1 tsp balsamic or red wine vinegar
    ½ tsp salt

Salsa can be served right away, but it's best to leave at room temperature for 1 hour to blend flavors. Because of tomatoes, salsa softens quickly, so make it the same day it is to be served. Refrigerate if not serving within an hour or two.

This salsa goes beautifully with burgers or Garlic-Rosemary Lamb Chops (see recipe page 89). You can also serve it on slices of Italian bread brushed with garlicky olive oil and lightly grilled, or spoon it over pasta and add freshly grated Parmesan.

Makes: 3 cups

PREPARATION: 10 MINUTES

BLACK BEAN 'N' PEPPER SALSA

Lime and hot peppers make this salsa an irresistible salad as well as a steak or burger topper.

In a large bowl, combine
    2 cups cooked black beans
      or a 19-oz can black beans, drained
    2 celery stalks, coarsely chopped
    1 sweet red pepper, coarsely chopped
    ½ unpeeled English cucumber, diced
    4 green onions, sliced
    1 to 2 hot banana or jalapeño peppers,
      seeded and finely chopped

Whisk together
    2 tbsp olive oil
    ⅓ cup freshly squeezed lime juice
    ½ tsp salt
    ¼ tsp freshly ground black pepper
    pinch of cayenne pepper (optional)

Pour over bean mixture. Gently mix, using a folding motion to avoid crushing beans. Taste and add more lime juice if you like. Can be served right away, but to blend flavors, let sit at room temperature for at least 1 hour before serving. Covered, salsa can be stored for up to 2 days in the refrigerator. Serve with Terrific Thai Steak (see recipe page 16).

Makes: 5 cups

PREPARATION: 10 MINUTES
MARINATE: 1 HOUR

Tomato & Hot Pepper Salsa

SAUCES & SALSAS

GARLIC-CHIVE SAUCE

This is the ultimate butter sauce for fish. Drizzle a little over the fish as soon as it comes off the grill.

In a small frying pan over medium heat, simmer
    ½ cup unsalted butter
    6 crushed garlic cloves
    until soft, at least 5 minutes.
    Don't let garlic brown.
Stir in
    ¼ cup chicken broth
    2 tbsp freshly squeezed lemon juice
    2 tbsp finely chopped chives or green onions
    ½ tsp freshly ground white or black pepper
    generous pinches of salt
    Heat through.
Serve warm, stirring just before serving.
    Makes: ¾ cup

PREPARATION: 5 MINUTES
COOK: 5 MINUTES

LEMON-CAPER SAUCE

A fast, yet sensational, sauce for grilled salmon or any fish steak.

In a small bowl, stir together
    ½ cup light sour cream
    2 tbsp finely chopped dill
    1 tbsp finely chopped capers
    1 tbsp freshly squeezed lemon or lime juice
    ½ tsp granulated sugar
    pinch of freshly ground white pepper
    pinch of salt (optional)
Covered and refrigerated, sauce will keep well for 2 days. This light low-cal cream sauce is wonderful spooned over top of any grilled fish or chicken. Also great as a dipping sauce for shrimp.
    Makes: ⅔ cup

PREPARATION: 5 MINUTES

OLIVE-TOMATO SALSA

For a sophisticated touch, spoon this versatile salsa over veal chops, halibut steaks, even chicken burgers.

In a medium-size bowl, stir together
    3 ripe tomatoes, seeded and chopped
    ¼ cup thinly sliced whole green onions
    2 tbsp slivered black olives
    1 tbsp minced jalapeño pepper
    1 crushed garlic clove
    3 tbsp good-quality olive oil
    1 tbsp red wine vinegar
    ½ tsp granulated sugar
    pinch of salt and ground black pepper
Taste and add more salt and pepper if you wish. Use right away or refrigerate, covered, up to a day. Because of tomatoes, salsa softens quickly, so make it the same day it is to be served.
    Makes: 1½ cups

PREPARATION: 15 MINUTES

FIERY BBQ SAUCE

Quickly wake up any barbecue sauce with these gusto stir-ins.

In a small bowl, stir together
    ¼ cup barbecue sauce
    2 tbsp Dijon mustard
    2 tsp Worcestershire sauce
    ¼ tsp hot pepper sauce
    ⅛ to ¼ tsp cayenne pepper
Use on burgers, wings, steak or chicken. Covered and refrigerated, sauce will keep well for at least a week.
    Makes: ½ cup

PREPARATION: 5 MINUTES

PRAIRIE BBQ SAUCE

Besides steak, this sauce is wonderful with sausages, chops, ribs and burgers.
Make up a batch and freeze some for later.

In a large saucepan set over medium heat, heat
    2 tbsp vegetable oil

Add
    2 onions, finely chopped
    1 green pepper, finely chopped
    2 crushed garlic cloves
    1 tbsp chili powder
    1 tsp ground cumin

Cook, stirring frequently, until onions are soft,
    about 5 minutes.

Stir in
    28-oz (796-mL) can undrained diced
      tomatoes
    ½ cup ketchup
    2 tbsp brown sugar
    2 tbsp Worcestershire sauce

Bring sauce to a boil. Reduce heat and simmer, covered, for 20 minutes to blend flavors. Stir often, especially when sauce begins to thicken. For a smooth sauce, whirl in a food processor. Use right away or refrigerate in a sealed jar, where it will keep for at least 1 week. Or freeze. To avoid burning, do not brush on steaks, chicken or ribs until the last 15 minutes of grilling time. Then serve extra for lavishly spooning over top.

Makes: 5 cups

> PREPARATION: 20 MINUTES
> COOK: 25 MINUTES

PRAIRIE BBQ SAUCE

SAUCES & SALSAS

Tangy Citrus Barbecue Sauce

Orange and lemon juices add tang to this not-so-sweet fresh-tasting barbecue sauce.

In a large saucepan, heat
   1/4 cup vegetable oil
Stir in
   2 onions, finely chopped
   4 crushed garlic cloves
   1 tbsp Dijon or other prepared mustard
   1 tsp dried leaf thyme
   1 tsp ground ginger
   1 tsp ground cumin
   1 tsp freshly ground black pepper
   1 tsp hot red pepper flakes
   2 bay leaves
   Cook over medium heat, uncovered, stirring often until onions soften, about 5 minutes.
Then stir in
   1 cup orange juice
   1 cup ketchup
   1/4 cup freshly squeezed lemon juice
   2 tbsp Worcestershire sauce
   2 tbsp soy sauce
   1 tbsp sugar
Bring to a simmer, then reduce heat to low. Cook, uncovered, stirring often as sauce thickens, about 20 minutes. For best flavor, cover and refrigerate for at least 1 day. Sauce will keep well, covered and refrigerated, for up to 1 week. Slather on chicken burgers or ribs near the end of barbecuing for a luscious coating.
Makes: 2 cups

> PREPARATION: 20 MINUTES
> COOK: 25 MINUTES

Salsa Italiano

Whip up this delicious salsa and use on grilled sausage or chicken. Great with creamy potato salad.

In a medium-size bowl, combine
   6 ripe tomatoes, seeded and chopped
   3 green onions, thinly sliced
   4 crushed garlic cloves
   3 tbsp olive oil
   1 tbsp balsamic vinegar
   1 tbsp finely chopped hot pepper,
      such as jalapeño
   1/2 tsp dried Italian seasoning
   generous pinches of salt and pepper
To give flavors a chance to blend, leave at room temperature for 1 hour. Drain well before serving. Tomatoes cause salsa to soften quickly, so make it the same day it is to be served. Covered and refrigerated, sauce will keep well for at least a day.
Makes: 4 cups

> PREPARATION: 15 MINUTES
> MARINATE: 1 HOUR

Peanut Sauce

Fresh ginger gives a zing to homemade peanut sauce. Wonderful with chicken kebabs or pork tenderloin.

In a small saucepan, combine
   1/3 cup smooth peanut butter
   1/3 cup chicken or vegetable broth
   1 tbsp brown sugar
   1 tbsp lime juice
   1 tbsp light soy sauce
   2 tsp grated fresh ginger
   pinch of hot red pepper flakes
Cook over medium heat, stirring often, until smooth and thickened, about 6 minutes. Set aside to cool. Refrigerated, it will keep well for several days.
Makes: 2/3 cup

> COOK: 6 MINUTES

MEXICANA SALSA

Team this corn-and-hot pepper mix with anything you want to add a south-of-the border flair to.

In a small bowl, stir together
  12-oz (341-mL) can drained kernel corn
    or 1 cup cooked frozen corn kernels
  2 ripe tomatoes, seeded and coarsely
    chopped
  2 tbsp chopped green chilies
    or jalapeño pepper
  2 tbsp finely chopped parsley
  1 tbsp freshly squeezed lime juice
  $\frac{1}{2}$ tsp ground cumin
Use right away or refrigerate until ready to use.
  Because of tomatoes, salsa softens quickly, so
  make it the same day it is to be served.
  Makes: 1½ cups

  PREPARATION: 15 MINUTES

TAPENADE

This olive spread from Provence is sublime on fish steaks, veal chops or chèvre-covered crackers.

In a food processor, whirl
  1 cup pitted black olives, such as kalamata
  2 drained anchovy fillets (optional)
  1 tbsp drained capers
  2 tbsp freshly squeezed lemon juice
  2 tbsp brandy
  1 tbsp olive oil
  1 tsp Dijon mustard
  1 tsp chopped fresh thyme
    or $\frac{1}{4}$ tsp dried leaf thyme
  $\frac{1}{4}$ tsp freshly ground black pepper
Scrape down sides as needed, until finely
chopped. Covered and refrigerated, tapenade
will keep well for up to 1 week.
  Makes: ¾ cup

  PREPARATION: 15 MINUTES

TIPS

Saucy Talk

- If a sauce is high in sugar, wait until the last few minutes of grilling to baste. The higher the sugar content the faster it will burn.

- If using a store-bought barbecue sauce, baste chicken, fish or ribs with oil at the beginning of the grilling, then thickly coat with the sauce for the last 5 to 10 minutes.

- When making your own sauce, be sure to add a little oil. It not only lubricates the food and keeps it from drying out, it helps prevent burning and sticking to the grill.

- Sauces should be fairly smooth. If not, simply purée in a blender or food processor.

Marinade Magic

- To tenderize a tough cut of meat, the marinade has to contain a liquid that's high in acid such as wine, tomato, lime or lemon juice or vinegar.

- An ideal dish for marinating is a glass or ceramic one that snugly holds the meat. A self-sealing bag is also good. The marinade should completely surround the meat.

- Don't use leftover marinade as a dipping or basting sauce unless you boil it for 5 minutes to destroy any bacteria contamination.

- To avoid bacteria contamination, most foods should be marinated in the refrigerator even though room temperature marinating is faster. It's fine, however, to leave a large piece of meat such as lamb, beef or roast at room temperature for an hour.

VEGETABLES

Vegetables take on a special flavor when they're grilled on the barbecue. The veggies in this LUSTY POTATO SALAD WITH MUSHROOMS & PEPPERS (see recipe page 122) are no exception, creating what is sure to be the most sensational potato salad you've ever tossed.

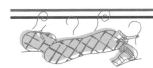

VEGETABLES

BARBECUED RATATOUILLE

Steam garden-fresh ratatouille in neat foil packets right on the barbecue next to your main course.

Preheat barbecue. In a large bowl, combine
 2 tbsp olive oil
 1 to 2 large crushed garlic cloves
 generous pinches of ground thyme,
  oregano, salt and black pepper
Add and toss until evenly coated
 2 medium-size zucchini, sliced into
  ¼-inch (0.5-cm) rounds
 2 firm tomatoes, sliced into 1-inch
  (2.5-cm) wedges
 1 small onion, finely chopped
 1 cup diced, peeled eggplant (optional)
 ½ green pepper, chopped (optional)
Place mixture in the centre of two large pieces of
  heavy foil. Push
 1 bay leaf
 into the middle of each mixture. Wrap tightly
 and press down to flatten slightly. Place on
 the grill and barbecue just until heated
 through, about 15 to 20 minutes. Turn the
 package every 5 minutes to ensure even
 heating.
Makes: 4 servings

PREPARATION: 10 MINUTES
GRILL: 20 MINUTES

BARBECUED SQUASH

Grilled squash slices take on a most appealing caramelized taste.

Make a small slit in skin of
 1 acorn or other medium-size squash
 Microwave on high until it can be pierced
 with a fork, 4 to 5 minutes.
 Slice in half. Remove seeds. Slice into
 ½-inch (1-cm) thick rounds.
Brush with
 olive oil or melted butter
Oil grill and preheat barbecue. Place squash on
 grill. Close lid and barbecue until grill marks
 appear and squash is tender, about 2 to 4
 minutes per side. Turn often.
Makes: 4 servings

PREPARATION: 15 MINUTES
MICROWAVE: 5 MINUTES
GRILL: 8 MINUTES

SWEET GRILLED PARSNIPS

Parsnips are a most unexpected vegetable for the barbie, but they sweeten up nicely on the grill.

Peel and slice in half
 parsnips
Brush with a mixture of
 sesame oil or melted butter
 olive oil
Then lightly sprinkle with
 coarse salt
Barbecue over medium heat, with the lid down,
 until golden and as soft as you like, about 5 to
 8 minutes per side. Parsnips are terrific with
 barbecued pork chops and chicken.

PREPARATION: 10 MINUTES
GRILL: 16 MINUTES

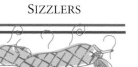

SMOKY CORN ON THE COB

Use our seasoned butter baste to enliven fresh corn on the cob.

Oil grill and preheat barbecue. Peel down husks just until silk can be discarded from

6 ears of corn, with husks

Pull husks back up. Place corn in a large bowl or saucepan. Cover with water and soak for 15 minutes. Then grill drained wet corn for about 25 minutes. Turn often and watch carefully.

Meanwhile, prepare peppery butter by stirring together

½ cup butter, at room temperature
¼ tsp freshly ground black pepper
¼ tsp chili powder
¼ tsp ground white pepper
¼ tsp cayenne pepper (optional)
¼ tsp salt

Use right away or cover and refrigerate for up to 1 week.

Remove corn and discard husks. Return corn to grill and cook, turning often, for 5 more minutes, so corn will pick up a smoky taste. Serve with peppery butter.

Makes: 6 servings

PREPARATION: 15 MINUTES
GRILL: 30 MINUTES

SMOKY CORN ON THE COB

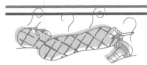

VEGETABLES

WARM TOMATO & FETA SALAD

If you like Greek salad, you'll adore this grilled version. It makes a stylish vegetarian entrée.

Oil grill and preheat barbecue. Place on grill
  8 whole tomatoes, ripe but firm
Lightly brush with
  1 to 2 tbsp olive oil
Turn frequently until tomato skins are lightly charred, about 10 to 12 minutes. Tomato skins will break during barbecuing.
Meanwhile, shred
  1 head romaine lettuce
and place on a serving platter or in a bowl. Sprinkle with
  2 whole green onions, thinly sliced
Then, in a small bowl, whisk together
  1/3 cup olive oil
  3 tbsp balsamic or red wine vinegar
  2 to 3 crushed garlic cloves
  1 tsp dried leaf oregano
  generous pinches of salt and
    freshly ground black pepper
When tomatoes are hot, remove to a cutting board. Coarsely chop or cut into wedges. Scatter over lettuce. Immediately sprinkle with
  1 cup crumbled feta cheese
Then drizzle with olive oil mixture and sprinkle with
  1/4 cup finely chopped fresh basil (optional)
Toss and serve immediately.
Makes: 4 to 6 servings

PREPARATION: 15 MINUTES
GRILL: 12 MINUTES

PESTO TOMATOES

Remember this idea when you want a no-work companion for any grilled entrée.

Oil grill and preheat barbecue. Slice in half
  2 large tomatoes, ripe but firm
Hold cut-side down and gently squeeze out some of the juice and seeds without altering the shape of tomatoes too much.
Place tomatoes cut-side down on grill. As soon as grill marks appear, after 5 minutes, turn with a wide spatula. On each, place a dab of
  pesto, homemade or store-bought
Gently spread. Continue grilling until sides of tomatoes feel warm, about 3 to 5 more minutes. Remove to a warm platter. Wonderful with steak or burgers.
Makes: 2 to 4 servings

PREPARATION: 5 MINUTES
GRILL: 10 MINUTES

HERBED CHÈVRE TOMATOES

For a change from plain sliced tomatoes, serve this warm chèvre number. Great with lamb.

Oil grill and preheat barbecue. Thickly slice
  2 tomatoes
Brush with
  1 tbsp olive oil
Sprinkle with
  1/4 tsp dried leaf oregano
  1/4 tsp dried basil
  freshly ground black or cayenne pepper
Place on grill and barbecue until hot, about 3 minutes per side. Top with
  2 tbsp crumbled feta or goat's cheese
Makes: 4 servings

PREPARATION: 5 MINUTES
GRILL: 6 MINUTES

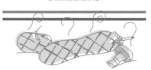

GRILLED CHEESE WITH TOMATO

Bread picks up a wonderful smoky flavor when barbecued. Add tomato, avocado and cheese for a main-course sandwich.

Oil grill and preheat barbecue. Thickly slice
   3 large tomatoes, ripe but firm
Slice into thin wedges
   1 avocado, peeled
Brush
   8 slices Italian bread, about ¾ inch
     (2 cm) thick
with
   1 to 2 tbsp melted butter, garlic butter
     or olive oil
Place tomatoes on hottest part of grill. Barbecue
   until grill marks appear, 1 to 3 minutes per side.
   Grill bread over cooler part of barbecue until
   underside is lightly toasted, from 1 to 3 minutes.

Turn over and top four of the toasted sides with
   Fontina or provolone cheese slices
Grill until underside is toasted, about 3 more
   minutes. Remove to plates. Layer tomatoes,
   lettuce and avocado on top of cheese. Add a
   dollop of
   Dijonnaise
and remaining slice of bread. Gently press
   sides together and serve right away.
Makes: 4 large sandwiches

> PREPARATION: 10 MINUTES
> GRILL: 12 MINUTES

GRILLED CHEESE WITH TOMATO

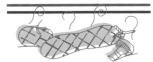

LUSTY POTATO SALAD WITH MUSHROOMS & PEPPERS

Grill or roast potatoes and peppers until flavors are enhanced. Then toss with meaty portobello mushrooms and blue cheese in a lime dressing.

Slice in half lengthwise

 6 medium-size new potatoes

 Then partially cook by boiling in water for 10 minutes or microwave, uncovered, on high, from 10 to 12 minutes. Oil grill and preheat barbecue.

Whisk together

 3 tbsp olive oil

 1 tsp paprika

 Generously brush potatoes with paprika mixture and place on hot grill.

Wrap in foil

 6 large peeled garlic cloves

 and place on grill. Turn garlic often until they soften, about 15 to 20 minutes.

Slice in half and remove stems and seeds from

 4 sweet peppers, a mix of colors

 2 banana peppers or 4 large jalapeño peppers (optional)

 Brush with paprika mixture, as well as on

 ¾ lb (375 g) large portobello mushrooms

After potatoes have been grilling about 5 minutes, add peppers. Turn several times until the pepper edges are just charred, about 10 minutes, and potatoes are golden, about 20 minutes. When vegetables are almost done, place mushrooms on barbecue. Grill just until mushrooms are hot and marked with grill marks on both sides, about 5 minutes. Remove vegetables from grill as soon as they are cooked.

Immediately slice hot potatoes into bite-size pieces and place in a bowl. Immediately crumble over top

 ½ cup crumbled blue cheese

  or ⅓ cup grated Parmesan

Gently stir so cheese softens and starts to melt. Slice peppers into bite-size pieces and add to potatoes. Thickly slice mushrooms, but do not add.

Stir together

 3 to 4 tbsp lime or lemon juice

  or red wine vinegar

 1 tbsp chopped fresh oregano

  or ½ tsp dried leaf oregano

 2 to 4 tbsp chopped fresh basil

  or ½ tsp dried basil

 ¼ tsp salt

 ¼ tsp freshly ground black pepper

Unwrap garlic and add hot cloves to lime juice mixture. Mash garlic as much as possible. Immediately pour over hot vegetables and toss. Stir in mushrooms.

Makes: 10 cups

PREPARATION: 25 MINUTES
MICROWAVE: 12 MINUTES
GRILL: 25 MINUTES

VARIATION: Grill a steak, about ¾ to 1 lb (375 to 500 g), until done as you like. Slice diagonally into thin strips and stir into salad in place of, or in addition to, the cheese.

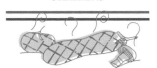

GRILLED MIXED PEPPER SALAD

Grilled peppers develop a sweetness far removed from the firm pieces on a crudités tray.

Oil grill and preheat barbecue. Seed and halve
  6 large sweet peppers, a mix of colors
Stir together
  2 tbsp olive oil
  3 minced garlic cloves
  Brush over peppers and
  1 small red onion, thickly sliced into rings
  Grill, turning once, until tender and lightly charred on edges, about 5 to 10 minutes.
Stir into remaining garlic-oil mixture
  4 tsp balsamic vinegar
  ¼ tsp salt
  ¼ tsp pepper
Then slice hot grilled peppers into ¼-inch (0.5-cm) strips and separate onion into rings.

Stir warm vegetables into olive oil mixture. Taste and add 1 tsp more vinegar if needed.
Stir in
¼ cup shredded fresh basil
12 oz (360 g) bocconcini cheese sliced into bite-size strips or 1 to 1½ cups coarsely shredded Asiago cheese
This is wonderful served with garlic bread grilled on the barbecue or chicken, fish, steak or burgers.
Makes: 7 cups, about 6 to 8 servings

PREPARATION: 15 MINUTES
GRILL: 10 MINUTES

GRILLED PEPPERS

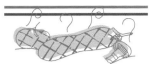

EASY GRILLED BALSAMIC PEPPERS

Tart up peppers with designer vinegar and sprinkles of paprika before grilling.

Stir together
 1 tbsp each olive oil and balsamic vinegar
 pinches of paprika, salt and freshly ground
 black pepper
Brush on
 3 sweet peppers, preferably a mix of colors,
 seeded and quartered
Grill, brushing with oil mixture occasionally,
 until hot and singed around the edges, about
 6 minutes per side. Good with barbecued
 chicken or juicy veal chops.
Makes: 2 to 3 servings

PREPARATION: 5 MINUTES
GRILL: 12 MINUTES

BBQ SWEET PEPPERS

*Here's a sure-fire method for grilling peppers
for sandwiches, sauces or roasted pepper soup.*

Slice in half lengthwise and discard seeds from
 large sweet peppers
Brush peppers with
 vegetable or olive oil
 Place on a hot grill and barbecue until skins
 have blackened a little. Turn often. This will
 take anywhere from 12 to 20 minutes.
Then to loosen skins a little so they are easy to
 peel off, remove peppers from grill and place
 in a bowl and cover with plastic wrap. Leave
 for at least 5 minutes. Peel off skin. Place on
 burgers before topping with buns.

PREPARATION: 2 MINUTES
GRILL: 20 MINUTES

INDOOR SIZZLE: *Oven Broiling*
Broil peppers on a baking sheet,
 turning often, until blistered on all
sides, about 10 to 15 minutes.

GRILLED GARLIC VEGETABLES

*A grilled mélange of fennel, sweet onion, potatoes
and pepper will stylishly round out any dinner.*

Keeping root end intact to hold layers together,
 slice lengthwise into quarters
 1 Vidalia or red onion, peeled
Cut in half lengthwise
 4 potatoes
Place, cut-side down, on paper towel in the
 microwave. Position so thickest part of
 potatoes are around outside of turntable.
 Place onion in centre of potatoes. Microwave,
 uncovered, on high, 10 minutes.
Meanwhile, seed and slice into quarters
 2 large red or yellow peppers
 Slice lengthwise into ½-inch (1-cm) strips
 1 large or 2 thin zucchini
 Remove feathery tops from
 1 large fennel bulb
 and slice lengthwise into quarters. Slice
 potato halves lengthwise to form slices no
 more than ¾ inch (2 cm) thick. Combine all
 vegetables in a bowl.
Stir together, then drizzle over vegetables
 ¼ cup olive oil
 2 crushed garlic cloves
 pinches of salt and freshly ground black
 pepper
 Toss until coated.
Barbecue until potatoes and onions are golden,
 about 10 minutes per side. Cook peppers,
 fennel and zucchini until tender, about 3 to
 7 minutes per side. As each vegetable is done,
 remove to a heated platter. Cover with foil to
 keep warm until all vegetables are grilled.
Makes: 4 generous servings

PREPARATION: 30 MINUTES
MICROWAVE: 10 MINUTES
GRILL: 20 MINUTES

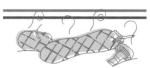

THYME ROSEMARY VEGETABLES

Smoky and tender-crisp from grilling, this mixture of everyday vegetables is most seductive.

Oil grill and preheat barbecue. Cut in half and seed
  3 sweet peppers, a mix of colors
Cut lengthwise into ¼-inch (0.5-cm) slices
  2 large zucchini
Cut into 1-inch (2.5-cm) slices
  1 large onion, preferably red or Vidalia
Clean
  10 very large mushrooms
Whisk together
  2 tbsp olive oil
  2 tbsp balsamic vinegar
  1 crushed garlic clove
  ¾ tsp finely chopped fresh rosemary or
    ¼ tsp crushed dried rosemary
  ¾ tsp finely chopped fresh thyme or
    ¼ tsp dried leaf thyme
  ½ tsp salt
  ¼ tsp freshly ground black pepper

Brush over vegetables. Grill until tender-crisp, about 10 minutes for zucchini and mushrooms, and 20 minutes for peppers and onions. Brush often with dressing. Remove from grill as veggies are done.

Slice hot vegetables into bite-size pieces and combine in a large bowl with
  ½ cup black or green olives (optional)
Drizzle with remaining dressing and toss. Taste and add more seasonings if needed. Serve warm. Salad will keep well, covered, in the refrigerator for up to 2 days. For a great pasta, warm leftovers in a frying pan or microwave with olive oil and chopped tomatoes.

Makes: 6 cups

PREPARATION: 15 MINUTES
GRILL: 20 MINUTES

GRILLED LEEKS

Grilled leeks are wonderful with such sophisticated entrées as grilled pork tenderloins or lamb chops.

Carefully trim roots from
  4 to 8 thin leeks
  so root bases remain intact to hold leeks together. Discard tough outer leaves. Slice off and discard dark green tops, leaving no more than 2 inches (5 cm) of light green portion. Cut in half lengthwise. Then gently spread out leaves and hold, root-end up, under cold running water to remove all grit.

To speed up cooking on grill, cook leeks, covered in gently boiling water in a wide frying pan, until they become a little brighter in color and just begin to soften, about 3 to 4 minutes. Or precook leeks in microwave on high just until they brighten a little in color. Start by microwaving 4 leeks for 2 minutes. If not barbecuing right away, plunge leeks into cold water to stop cooking and refrigerate.

In a small bowl, whisk together
  3 tbsp olive or vegetable oil
  2 small crushed garlic cloves
  pinch of hot red pepper flakes
    or cayenne pepper

Oil grill and preheat barbecue. Pat leeks dry and generously brush with baste. Place on grill and barbecue, basting and turning occasionally, until they just begin to char, 6 to 8 minutes.

Makes: 2 to 4 servings

PREPARATION: 10 MINUTES
COOK: 4 MINUTES
GRILL: 8 MINUTES

VEGETABLES

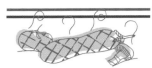

VEGETABLES

ZUCCHINI & CHILI SALSA

*When the garden groans with zucchini,
here's a delightful new way to serve it!*

Oil grill and preheat barbecue. Lightly brush with
olive or vegetable oil
  2 large zucchini, sliced lengthwise,
    about ½ inch (1 cm) thick
  2 sweet peppers, preferably 1 red and
    1 yellow, seeded and halved
  4 jalapeño, banana or other hot peppers,
    seeded and halved
  1 onion, cut in half crosswise
Grill until vegetables are lightly browned,
turning once, about 5 minutes for hot
peppers, 10 minutes for zucchini, 15 minutes
for sweet peppers and 20 minutes for onions.
Remove vegetables as they are done.
Finely chop vegetables and place in a mixing
bowl. Stir in
  3 tbsp freshly squeezed lime juice,
    about 2 limes
  ¼ cup chopped fresh coriander
  ½ tsp salt
Let stand at room temperature for at least 30
minutes to develop flavors. Taste and stir in
more lime juice if needed. Salsa can be
covered and refrigerated for up to 2 days, but
bring to room temperature before serving.
Wonderful with barbecued chicken or fish,
or over fajitas.
Makes: 3¼ cups

*PREPARATION: 15 MINUTES
MARINATE: 30 MINUTES
GRILL: 20 MINUTES*

BBQ TOSSED SALAD

*Barbecued veggies meet crisp fresh greens
in this grilled salad.*

Oil grill and preheat barbecue. Brush with
olive oil
  2 small zucchini, cut lengthwise
    into ¼-inch (0.5-cm) slices
  3 sweet peppers, a mix of colors,
    seeded and halved
  4 large whole green onions
Place on grill and barbecue for 8 to 12
minutes, turning frequently, just until
vegetables are tender-crisp.
Meanwhile, tear into bite-size pieces and place in
a large bowl
  1 head romaine lettuce or 1 small romaine
    and 1 small soft-leaf lettuce
Whisk together
  3 tbsp red wine vinegar
  2 tsp Dijon mustard
  1 tsp dried basil
  ½ tsp leaf oregano
  pinch of salt
  generous grinding of black pepper
Gradually whisk in
  ¼ cup olive oil
Dressing will be quite vinegary.
Once vegetables are cooked, slice into bite-size
pieces and immediately toss with dressing.
Turn hot vegetables over lettuce, toss and
serve. If making ahead, you can leave the
grilled vegetables at room temperature for
several hours. Keep lettuce in refrigerator
until ready to toss with vegetables.
Makes: 4 servings

*PREPARATION: 15 MINUTES
GRILL: 12 MINUTES*

TIPS

BBQ Veggie Basics

- To make the most of glorious garden produce, grill vegetables on the barbie alongside chicken or ribs. They'll take on an irresistible smoky taste, so you won't need to smear on a lot of butter. To prevent sticking and to keep vegetables moist, lightly baste with olive oil or melted butter before grilling. Turn often.

Grill Exra

- Toss extra veggies on the barbecue. Slice hot veggies into bite-size pieces. Toss with garlicky olive oil, balsamic vinegar and chopped fresh basil or your favorite salad dressing. Refrigerate and serve cold as a salad or mix with tossed greens.

- Refrigerate or freeze extra grilled tomato halves. For a roasted tomato soup, whirl in a food processor with garlic.

SMART GRILLED VEGGIES

Corn on the Cob
Wrap in foil and grill for 20 to 25 minutes, turning often.
Flavor boosts: butter with crushed red pepper, cayenne, cumin or chopped chives.

Eggplant
Slice lengthwise. Sprinkle with salt, then oil. Grill until soft, 12 to 15 minutes, turning often.
Flavor boosts: baste with salad dressing or garlic- or herb-flavored oils. Top with fresh tomato salsa.

Mushrooms
Thread onto skewers. Brush with olive oil, sesame oil or melted butter. Grill for 4 to 7 minutes, turning often.
Flavor boosts: sprinkle with dill, rosemary or chives.

Peppers
Slice into halves or quarters. Seed and brush with oil. Grill until they start to char, about 10 to 12 minutes, turning often.
Flavor boosts: garlic oil or Italian salad dressing.

Potatoes
Bake in a 350°F (180°C) oven for 30 minutes. Thickly slice. Baste with oil. Grill until hot and golden, about 15 minutes.
Flavor boosts: melt 2 tbsp butter with 1 crushed garlic clove and ¼ tsp freshly ground black pepper. Add a pinch of cayenne, chili powder and cumin if you like. Brush over ¼-inch (0.5-cm) thick potato slices on grill.

Zucchini
Thickly slice lengthwise. Brush with butter or oil. Grill until hot, about 6 minutes, turning often.
Flavor boosts: melted butter with garlic and basil, tarragon or curry powder added.

XTRAS

Basil-scented UPTOWN BARBECUED PIZZA (see recipe page 130)
is a perfect BBQ appetizer. Keep a pizza crust in the freezer,
top with grilled peppers and creamy goat's cheese and
this sophisticated pizza is yours in less than 20 minutes.

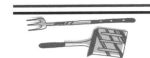

UPTOWN BARBECUED PIZZA

Grill pizza in less time than it takes for the delivery guy to arrive.

Oil grill and preheat barbecue. Grill
  2 small red and yellow peppers
  turning often until blackened and blistered on all sides. Cool slightly, then peel, core and seed. Cut into julienne strips.
Brush both sides of
  10-inch (25-cm) round focaccia bread
    or store-bought baked pizza crust
  with
  2 tsp olive oil
  Place bottom-side up on grill and barbecue until grill marks appear, about 2 to 4 minutes. Watch to make sure it does not burn. Turn.
Immediately sprinkle over top of hot focaccia
  ¼ lb (125 g) crumbled creamy goat cheese
  2 tbsp finely chopped fresh basil
  ¼ tsp black pepper
  Then scatter roasted pepper strips over top. Grill until golden on bottom and cheese starts to melt, about 2 to 4 minutes. Carefully watch to prevent burning. Cut into wedges and serve.
Makes: 6 wedges, about 2 dinner servings
  or 6 appetizers

PREPARATION: 10 MINUTES
GRILL: 8 MINUTES

INDOOR SIZZLE: *Oven Broiling*
Preheat broiler. Place whole peppers on a foil-lined baking sheet, about 4 inches (10 cm) from broiler. Broil peppers until blackened and blistered on all sides, about 10 minutes. Proceed as above to peel peppers. Then broil oiled focaccia bottom-side up until lightly toasted. Turn and add cheese as above. Continue grilling until cheese starts to melt. Add remaining toppings and serve.

GRILLED VEGETARIAN SANDWICHES

This creation makes you realize a sandwich can sometimes be more exciting than a classic entrée.

Oil grill and preheat barbecue. Slice lengthwise
  about ⅓ inch (0.8 cm) thick
  2 slim Japanese eggplants
    or 1 round unpeeled Sicilian eggplant
Whisk together
  ¼ cup olive oil
  ¼ cup red wine vinegar
  ½ cup finely chopped fresh basil
  2 crushed garlic cloves
  ½ tsp salt
  Brush over eggplant and place on grill. Barbecue for 3 to 5 minutes per side, basting occasionally with basil mixture, until eggplant is well browned.
Slice in half
  2 pieces focaccia bread
  Heat on grill until lightly toasted, about 2 minutes per side. Layer several eggplant slices on focaccia bottoms, folding, if necessary, to fit. Top with
  slices of Asiago or Romano cheese,
    about ¼ lb (125 g)
  1 large tomato, thinly sliced
  fresh basil leaves
  Top with focaccia slices. Serve hot.
Makes: 2 large sandwiches

PREPARATION: 15 MINUTES
GRILL: 10 MINUTES

WARM GREEK SANDWICHES

This sandwich is a sensational use for feta! Add a glass of chilled white wine and you've got an impressive lunch. Great for weekend guests.

Oil grill and preheat barbecue. Thinly slice
  1 lb (500 g) feta cheese
  Slice horizontally
  2 long French baguettes
  then slice each half into 4 pieces.
Stir together
  ⅓ cup olive oil
  2 large crushed garlic cloves
Brush bread with oil mixture. Grill, cut-side down, until toasted, about 2 to 3 minutes. Turn bread and top with feta. Grill 2 to 3 minutes until grill marks start to appear on baguette and feta begins to melt.

Place on serving plates. Cover with
  4 sliced tomatoes
  24 fresh large basil leaves
Then drizzle with any remaining garlic oil.
Makes: 8 open-face sandwiches

PREPARATION: 10 MINUTES
GRILL: 6 MINUTES

INDOOR SIZZLE: *Oven Broiling*
 Place bread on a broiler pan about 4 inches (10 cm) from broiler. Broil until toasted, then top with cheese and broil until melted.

WARM GREEK SANDWICHES

XTRAS

GRILLED ITALIAN SANDWICH

Once you've had this sandwich, there's no turning back to a basic club.

Oil grill and preheat barbecue. Cut in half and seed
  2 sweet red peppers
  Pierce casings in several places of
  4 hot or sweet Italian sausages

Place sausages and peppers on grill. Close lid or cover with foil tent. Barbecue peppers, turning once or twice, until softened and slightly charred, about 12 to 18 minutes. Sausages should be turned often and barbecued until lightly browned, about 15 to 25 minutes.

Slice in half and warm on barbecue
  4 kaiser or onion buns
  Remove sausages and peppers from barbecue. Cut sausages, diagonally, into ½-inch (1-cm) slices. Remove skin from peppers if you wish.

Spread warm buns with
  creamy chèvre cheese
  Top with sausages and peppers.
Makes: 4 sandwiches

PREPARATION: 15 MINUTES
GRILL: 25 MINUTES

MANGO & CHILI QUESADILLAS

A tortilla wedge filled with Brie and mango stands out as an innovative barbecued appetizer.

Oil grill and preheat barbecue. Place
  2 sweet red peppers
  1 jalapeño or other hot pepper (optional)
  on grill and barbecue until outsides are partially blackened and skin is beginning to lift away, about 10 minutes.

In a bowl, place
  1 ripe mango, peeled and finely chopped
  ¼ cup chopped coriander
  When peppers are grilled, peel away any charred skin, then seed and finely chop. Stir into mango mixture.

On a counter, lay
  4 (10-inch/25-cm)
    or 8 (7-inch/18-cm) flour torillas
  Partially cover half of each tortilla with
  slices of Brie, Camembert or crumbled chèvre
  Do not try to cover whole surface. Spread with mango mixture.
  Squeeze over top a little
  lime juice

Fold uncovered side over filling. Brush both sides of tortilla with
  melted butter

Pick up filled tortilla by grasping open edges at opposite sides while supporting folded tortilla with your hands. Keep horizontal while placing on grill. Barbecue until golden grill marks appear on both sides of tortilla and cheese is just melted, about 1 to 2 minutes per side. Cut into wedges and serve.
Makes: 16 appetizer wedges

PREPARATION: 15 MINUTES
GRILL: 14 MINUTES

BASIL-SAUSAGE MEATBALLS

If there is such a thing as a gourmet meatball, this is it. Wrap in a tortilla or pita warmed on the grill or serve on spicy rice.

Oil grill and preheat barbecue. Remove from casings and place in a medium-size bowl
1 lb (500 g) sausage,
    preferably hot or sweet Italian
If using regular breakfast sausage, add
1 tsp Italian seasoning
Stir in
¼ cup bread crumbs
¼ cup finely chopped fresh basil
Form sausage meat into balls no more than
1 inch (2.5 cm) in diameter. Around each meatball wrap
1 whole large basil leaf

Don't worry if basil leaves do not completely wrap around meatballs.
Thread 3 basil-wrapped meatballs, each spaced about ½ inch (1 cm) apart, onto skewers. Place on a well-greased grill. Close lid or cover with foil tent and turn frequently until done, about 8 to 12 minutes.
Makes: 4 servings

PREPARATION: 20 MINUTES
GRILL: 12 MINUTES

XTRAS

BASIL-SAUSAGE MEATBALLS

XTRAS

SAUSAGE FAJITAS

For the ultimate in relaxed dining, try these yummy fajitas.

Oil grill and preheat barbecue. In a small bowl, stir together

7-oz (217-mL) can tomato sauce

¼ cup olive oil

1 crushed garlic clove

½ tsp ground coriander

½ tsp ground cumin

¼ tsp freshly ground black pepper

Pierce casings in several places of

4 sausages, such as Octoberfest or Italian
Place sausages on hot grill. Close lid or cover with foil tent. Barbecue sausages, turning often, until lightly browned, about 10 minutes.

Set aside ¾ cup of tomato mixture, then baste sausages with remaining sauce. Continue turning sausages, basting often, until richly glazed, about 10 more minutes.

Into reserved tomato sauce, stir

1 fresh tomato, finely chopped

¼ cup chopped coriander or parsley

Place sausages on

4 flour tortillas

Top with tomato sauce, then

shredded lettuce

sour cream

Roll tortillas around sausages.
Makes: 4 servings

PREPARATION: 20 MINUTES
GRILL: 20 MINUTES

SAUSAGES PROVENÇAL

These sausages go perfectly with a grilled vegetable or potato salad. Or wrap up in a crusty roll.

Oil grill and preheat barbecue. In a small bowl, stir together

¼ cup Dijon mustard

¼ cup liquid honey

1 tbsp white wine or apple juice

generous pinches of crushed dried rosemary, leaf thyme, savory and ground black pepper

Covered and refrigerated, sauce will keep for a week.

Pierce casings in several places of

4 large sausages, such as bratwurst or Italian

Place on hot grill. Close lid or cover with foil tent and barbecue, turning often, until lightly browned, about 10 minutes.

Then, baste sausages with sauce. Continue turning sausages, basting often, until richly glazed, about 10 to 15 more minutes. Serve sausages with remaining sauce for dipping.
Makes: 4 servings

PREPARATION: 15 MINUTES
GRILL: 25 MINUTES

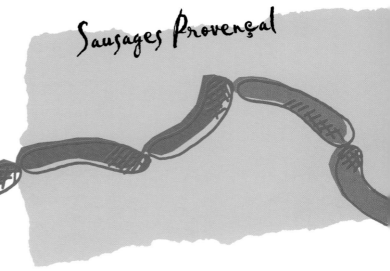

Sausages Provençal

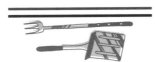

GLAZED CORNED BEEF

Expand your grilled entrée repertoire by blazing corned beef over the coals.

Oil grill and preheat barbecue. Tightly wrap in heavy foil
    1-lb (500-g) piece corned beef, not sliced
Place on grill and barbecue, lid closed, for 30 minutes, turning partway through.
Meanwhile, in a saucepan, heat
    ¼ cup apple jelly
    2 tbsp vegetable oil
    just until jelly is melted.
Whisk in
    2 tbsp Dijon mustard
    ½ tsp curry powder
    1 tbsp chopped fresh tarragon or
      ½ tsp dried tarragon
Remove meat from wrapping. Place on grill and generously brush with apple-jelly mixture. Barbecue, turning and brushing with mixture until brisket is richly glazed, about 3 minutes per side.
Makes: 6 servings

> *PREPARATION: 10 MINUTES*
> *COOK: 5 MINUTES*
> *GRILL: 36 MINUTES*

SUMMERTIME JAMBALAYA

Spicy jambalaya is a refreshing change of pace on a hot summer's eve.

Oil grill and preheat barbecue. In several places pierce casings of
    6 hot Italian sausages
Place sausages on grill. Close lid or cover with a foil tent. Barbecue, turning frequently, about 15 to 20 minutes.
Meanwhile, slice lengthwise into quarters
    3 sweet peppers, preferably a mix of colors
Slice lengthwise in half
    2 small hot banana peppers
Place peppers on grill and barbecue, turning frequently, just until lightly grilled, about 8 minutes.
In a large bowl, whisk together
    3 tbsp olive oil
    2 tbsp red wine vinegar
    3 crushed garlic cloves
    ¼ tsp hot pepper sauce
    1 tsp dried leaf thyme
    1 tsp dried leaf oregano
Stir in
    4 cups cooked rice
Stir constantly until all grains are coated. Add more seasonings if needed.
Slice in half and add to rice mixture
    1½ cups cherry tomatoes, about 12
As soon as peppers are grilled, slice sweet peppers into bite-size pieces. Finely chop hot peppers and stir into rice.
When sausages are cooked, slice into ¼-inch (0.5 cm) pieces. Stir into jambalaya and serve immediately.
Makes: 8 servings

> *PREPARATION: 10 MINUTES*
> *GRILL: 20 MINUTES*

ZESTY CORNISH HENS

Grated lime and orange peel give a fast elegance to these little golden birds.

Place in a shallow dish just large enough to hold them or in a self-sealing bag
  2 Cornish hens, split in half lengthwise
Whisk together
  ¼ cup vegetable or olive oil
  finely grated peel and juice of
    1 orange and 1 lime
  1 green onion, finely chopped
  1 crushed garlic clove
  generous grinding of black pepper
  Pour about ⅔ of mixture over hens. Marinate at room temperature for 20 minutes or refrigerate about 2 hours. Turn once.
Preheat barbecue. Remove hens from marinade. Discard marinade. Place halves on individual pieces of heavy-duty foil. Seal tightly. Grill packets, 35 minutes, turning several times.
Then remove foil packets from grill. Place hens directly on grill. Brush with remaining citrus mixture. Barbecue, turning and basting every few minutes, until skin is golden and crisp, about 10 to 20 more minutes.
Makes: 2 servings

PREPARATION: 10 MINUTES
MARINATE: 20 MINUTES
GRILL: 55 MINUTES

CITRUS CORNISH HENS

Combine lemon and lime juice to give an island taste to elegant Cornish hens.

Finely grate peel from
  3 limes
  2 lemons
  1 orange
  and place in a small bowl. Squeeze enough juice from fruits so you have ¼ cup each of lime, lemon and orange juice. Pour over peel and whisk in
  ⅓ cup olive oil
  2 tsp dried leaf thyme or rosemary
  ¼ tsp cracked black or white pepper
Cut
  4 Cornish hens
  in half, lengthwise, along centre of breastbone and back. Place pieces, cut-side up, in a glass dish just large enough to hold them snugly. Add juice mixture. Cover and refrigerate for at least 1 hour, turning at least once, or overnight.
Oil grill and preheat barbecue. Remove hens from marinade. Discard marinade. Wrap each piece in 1 layer of foil. Barbecue for 35 to 45 minutes, turning often. Unwrap, remove from packets and barbecue right on the grill until browned, about 8 to 12 minutes, turning often.
Makes: 8 servings

PREPARATION: 20 MINUTES
MARINATE: 1 HOUR
GRILL: 57 MINUTES

GRILLED ROSEMARY VEAL

*The classic companions of quality olive oil, Dijon and rosemary
provide just enough flavored dressing for mild veal.*

Trim fat from
 4 veal chops, about ¾ inch (2 cm) thick
 Place in a dish just large enough to hold them snugly or in a self-sealing bag.
In a small dish, whisk together
 ¼ cup olive oil
 1 tbsp freshly squeezed lemon juice
 1 tbsp Dijon mustard
 1 tsp dried rosemary, crushed
 generous grindings of black pepper
Pour over chops, making sure they are coated evenly. Cover or seal and refrigerate for at least 1 hour or overnight. Turn chops at least once during this time.

Just before grilling, bring chops to room temperature. Oil grill and preheat barbecue. Remove chops from marinade and place on grill. Barbecue for 10 to 15 minutes, turning often. Veal chops are wonderful served with Roasted Red Pepper Sauce (see recipe page 108).
Makes: 4 servings

PREPARATION: 5 MINUTES
MARINATE: 1 HOUR
GRILL: 15 MINUTES

GRILLED ROSEMARY VEAL

XTRAS

SHERRIED VEAL CHOPS

Tender veal chops are pricey and deserve to be paired with sherry or marsala.

Trim excess fat from
  4 veal chops, 1 inch (2.5 cm) thick
  Place chops in a dish just large enough to hold them snugly or in a self-sealing bag.
Whisk together
  ¼ cup dry sherry or marsala
  ¼ cup vegetable oil
  4 crushed garlic cloves
  1 tsp Worcestershire sauce
  pinches of salt and black pepper
  Pour over chops. If using a dish, turn chops to coat evenly and cover, or seal plastic bag and place in a bowl.
Marinate at room temperature for 1 hour or refrigerate for at least 4 hours. Turn chops at least once during this time.
Then oil grill and preheat barbecue. Drain chops and place on grill. Barbecue 5 to 6 minutes per side, turning often.
Makes: 4 servings

PREPARATION: 5 MINUTES
MARINATE: 1 HOUR
GRILL: 12 MINUTES

ELEGANT PARMESAN VEAL ROLLS

Veal rolls ooze with warm Parmesan — the real thing — and Dijon in this special entrée.

Oil grill and preheat barbecue. Lay
  8 veal scallops, ¼ inch (0.5 cm) thick
  on a piece of waxed paper.
  Thinly spread with
  1 tbsp Dijon mustard
  Then generously sprinkle with
  ½ cup freshly grated Parmesan cheese

Tightly roll up each scallop and thread crosswise onto skewers. Do not crowd scallops on skewers. Leave a little space between each.
Whisk together
  ¼ cup vegetable oil
  3 tbsp freshly squeezed lemon juice
  generous pinches of salt and freshly ground white or black pepper
  Generously brush over scallops.
Place veal rolls on grill and barbecue, turning and brushing frequently with oil mixture, about 7 minutes per side.
Makes: 4 servings

PREPARATION: 15 MINUTES
GRILL: 14 MINUTES

LITE TARRAGON-TURKEY GRILL

Bathe lean turkey in a tarragon-white wine baste for an elegant low-fat entrée.

In a saucepan, combine
  1 cup white wine
  2 tbsp olive oil
  2 crushed garlic cloves
  2 tsp dried tarragon
  ¼ tsp salt
  Boil over medium heat, uncovered, until reduced to about ½ cup.
Oil grill and preheat barbecue. Baste sauce over
  4 turkey cutlets or ½-inch (1-cm) thick turkey-breast slices
  Place on hot grill and barbecue for 5 to 6 minutes per side, basting often with sauce, until turkey feels firm. Remove from the grill and pour any remaining sauce over hot turkey. Wonderful with wild rice or risotto.
Makes: 4 servings

PREPARATION: 5 MINUTES
GRILL: 12 MINUTES

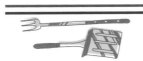

EASY GRILLED POLENTA

*Try polenta in place of potatoes
the next time you're grilling.*

Slice into ½-inch (1-cm) rounds
    2-lb (1-kg) roll of store-bought polenta
Brush with
    olive oil
Place on oiled grill. Grill, checking underside
    occasionally, until golden tinged and hot,
    about 15 to 20 minutes per side. Then
    sprinkle with
    Parmesan or Romano cheese
Makes: 6 to 8 servings

> PREPARATION: 5 MINUTES
> GRILL: 40 MINUTES

ZESTY LIVER

*Madame Bénoit first suggested using a spritz of
vinegar on liver — here it's taken to new heights.*

Oil grill and preheat barbecue. In a small bowl,
    whisk together
    ¼ cup red wine vinegar
    ¼ cup vegetable or olive oil
    3 crushed garlic cloves
Place
    4 pieces calf's liver, each about ¼ lb (125 g)
    on grill. Brush with garlic mixture and grill
    for about 5 to 8 minutes, turning once or
    twice during barbecuing. Serve with Pesto
    Tomatoes (see recipe page 120).
Makes: 4 servings

> PREPARATION: 5 MINUTES
> GRILL: 8 MINUTES

INDOOR SIZZLE: *Sauté*
Cook marinated liver in a frying
pan in 1 to 2 tbsp butter or oil over
medium heat, about 3 minutes per side.

HERBED GRILLED LIVER

*Lemon and rosemary go beautifully with liver.
Grill red onions for a perfect accompaniment.*

Place in a shallow glass dish just large enough to
    fit in a single layer or in a large self-sealing bag
    1 ½ lbs (750 g) calf's liver,
        sliced about ½ inch (1 cm) thick
In a small bowl, stir together
    ¼ cup good-quality olive oil
    1 tbsp lemon juice
    1 crushed garlic clove (optional)
    1 tsp finely grated lemon peel
    1 tsp dried rosemary
    ¼ tsp freshly ground black pepper
    Pour over liver. Seal and leave at room
    temperature for 1 hour or refrigerate for
    2 hours.
Oil grill and preheat barbecue. Place drained
    liver on grill and barbecue for about
    3 minutes per side. Liver should still have
    a slightly pink tinge. Accompany with grilled
    sliced onions or sliced tomatoes.
Makes: 4 servings

> PREPARATION: 10 MINUTES
> MARINATE: 1 HOUR
> GRILL: 6 MINUTES

INDOOR SIZZLE:
For stove-top sauté, see left.

Easy Grilled Polenta

139

CREDITS

ILLUSTRATIONS by Jeff Jackson

PHOTOGRAPHS

Ed O'Neil: front cover and pages 15, 17, 19, 35, 41, 45, 49, 51, 55, 57, 59, 71, 81, 87, 89, 103, 109, 113, 117, 119, 121

Michael Mahovlich: pages 2, 9, 11, 23, 29, 31, 61, 69, 75, 77, 95, 97, 101, 105, 123, 129, 133, 137

Michael Visser: pages 63, 131   Ed Eng: page 43   Bernard Leroux: page 91

Back cover photograph of Monda Rosenberg and the Chatelaine Test Kitchen staff by Susan Dobson.

CHATELAINE food express
Sizzlers

FOR SMITH SHERMAN BOOKS INC.

EDITORIAL DIRECTOR
Carol Sherman

ART DIRECTOR
Andrew Smith

SENIOR EDITOR
Bernice Eisenstein

EDITORIAL ASSISTANCE
Debra Sherman

DESIGN ASSISTANCE
Joseph Gisini

COLOR SEPARATIONS
Acuity Digital Imaging, Richmond Hill

PRINTING
Kromar Printing Ltd., Winnipeg

SMITH SHERMAN BOOKS INC.
657 Davenport Road, Toronto, Canada M5R 1L3
e-mail: bloke@total.net

FOR CHATELAINE

FOOD EDITOR
Monda Rosenberg

ASSOCIATE FOOD EDITOR
Marilyn Crowley

TEST KITCHEN ASSISTANT
Trudy Patterson

CHATELAINE ADVISORY BOARD
Rona Maynard, Lee Simpson

PROJECT MANAGER
Cheryl Smith

SPECIAL SALES
Mark Jones

CHATELAINE, MACLEAN HUNTER PUBLISHING
LIMITED
777 Bay Street, Toronto, Canada M5W 1A7
e-mail: letters@chatelaine.com

Look for other book titles in the CHATELAINE library

NEW TWISTS for 100 everyday foods from apples to zucchini. Includes a survival guide and a comprehensive index.

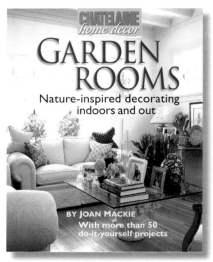

DECORATING INSPIRATION for every room of the house, including rooms for outdoor living and dining, with more than 50 easy do-it-yourself projects.